Worship Any Time
or Place

Worship Any Time or Place

The Compact Book of Methodist Liturgies, Prayers, and Other Acts of Blessing

Nelson Cowan, General Editor and Contributor

Abingdon Press,
Nashville, TN

WORSHIP ANY TIME OR PLACE

Copyright © 2023 by Abingdon Press

All rights reserved.

ISBN: 978-1-7910-2983-8

Library of Congress Control Number has been requested.

Scripture quotations unless noted otherwise are taken from the Common English Bible, copyright © 2011. Used by permission. All rights reserved.

Scripture quotations marked NRSVUE are taken from the New Revised Standard Version Updated Edition. Copyright © 2021 National Council of Churches of Christ in the United States of America. Used by permission. All rights reserved worldwide.

Scripture quotations marked ESV are from the ESV® Bible (The Holy Bible, English Standard Version®), copyright © 2001 by Crossway, a publishing ministry of Good News Publishers. Used by permission. All rights reserved.

Scripture quotations marked MSG are taken from THE MESSAGE, copyright © 1993, 1994, 1995, 1996, 2000, 2001, 2002 by Eugene H. Peterson. Used by permission of NavPress. All rights reserved. Represented by Tyndale House Publishers, Inc.

Scripture quotations marked (NIV) are taken from the Holy Bible, New International Version®, NIV®. Copyright © 1973, 1978, 1984, 2011 by Biblica, Inc.™ Used by permission of Zondervan. All rights reserved worldwide. www.zondervan.com The "NIV" and "New International Version" are trademarks registered in the United States Patent and Trademark Office by Biblica, Inc.™

See source list on pages 123-40 for permission notices and acknowledgments.

Every reasonable attempt has been made to secure permissions for quoted material. The publisher regrets any omission and will, upon notice, make necessary corrections in subsequent printings.

MANUFACTURED IN THE UNITED STATES OF AMERICA

CONTENTS

Contents

Contents

Contents

Contents

Contents

  * *The people called Methodists hold a diversity of theological perspectives.*
    This prayer may not be suitable for some contexts.

INTRODUCTION

Worship Any Time or Place is a compact collection of over 200 resources for corporate worship and personal devotion, intended for clergy and laity. For clergy, this volume contains resources for the administration of the sacraments, as well as funeral services and other "pastor-led" moments. The majority of resources, however, are suitable for laity. Some may serve in a variety of church leadership roles, such as worship planners and leaders, lay servants, liturgists, congregational care ministers, deaconesses and home missioners, and members of committees and leadership teams. Others may want these resources to expand and nurture their life of prayer as parents, teachers, business executives, neighbors, justice-seekers, caretakers, retirees—and all of God's people. *Worship Any Time or Place* equips these people to offer a steady, capable, prayerful voice to the myriad moments of life that take place between the Lord's Day and the rest of the week.

While this book has been compiled for the people called Methodists (e.g., AME, AMEZ, CME, Free Methodist, GMC, and UMC), it is ecumenical in scope. The source materials and contributors are intentionally diverse across theological traditions and perspectives, race, ethnicity, sexual orientation, and gender identity. *Worship Any Time or Place* offers further diversity by balancing prayer forms that are ancient and modern, formal and informal, scriptural and nonscriptural, straightforward and poetic. An English-language resource, this collection employs expansive language in referencing God and inclusive language in referencing humanity.

Worship Any Time or Place is inspired by the *Pastor's Pocket Edition of The United Methodist Book of Worship* (1992), which is primarily for clergy. *Worship Any Time or Place* empowers all voices, providing words of worship for both clergy and laity for moments that are official or unofficial; that are planned or spontaneous; that take place at churches, homes, or workplaces; that are needed for Sundays or any other day. Expect this book to carry some holy mementos: crumbs lodged into its spine from table blessings, earmarked pages from bedtime prayers, bits of gravel from protests, hand sanitizer stains from hospital visits, dirt marks from gardens or animals, torn pages from children at play, mascara-tinged teardrops from interpersonal prayers, coffee stains from still mornings, and frazzled pages from sitting in the sun. Since this book travels well, perhaps it might get lost during a journey, only for a stranger to find it as a blessing.

Any resource collection cannot be all things to all people. Due to the compact size of *Worship Any Time or Place*, not every prayer, liturgy, rite of passage, occasion, blessing, or worship service could be included. Gaps and omissions certainly exist. Perhaps these gaps and omissions invite you, readers, to create new prayers, liturgies, and other acts of blessing for the unique needs in your context, and to share them however you are able.

Above all, may the resources in this book inspire God's people to mark all instances of life with prayer, or as the Apostle Paul said: to "pray without ceasing" (1 Thessalonians 5:17). From pulpits to pews, from altar tables to dinner tables, from sanctuaries to streets, *Worship Any Time or Place* can be used by all ministers—clergy and laity—to employ worshipful words as the Spirit leads.

Rev. Nelson Robert Cowan, PhD, General Editor
The Nineteenth Week after Pentecost, 2023

HOW TO USE THIS BOOK

Worship Any Time or Place is a portable and adaptable collection of prayer resources for clergy and laity. It is approachable for all levels of experience—from seasoned pastoral leaders to newly appointed clergy, from decades-long office holders to emerging lay leaders, from Christians who were practically raised in the church to those who are in the beginning stages of faith. This book provides thoughtful words and set forms from which to pray at a moment's notice. Keep it close by at church, at work, in the car, and at home, ready to use whenever the need arises.

Part One: Structures and Seasons | This section offers foundational information about the basic pattern of worship, the liturgical year, and the timeless prayer form known as a collect. While Methodist in perspective, it is a succinct introduction to the shared faith and practices of multiple denominations and traditions.

Parts Two and Three constitute the bulk of the book and are organized by the time and place these resources are utilized, as well as by the principal liturgical leader.

Part Two: Worship on the Lord's Day | These resources are primarily intended for use on Sunday and/or the principal day of worship for a faith community. In the Table of Contents, they are organized by function within a service of worship (i.e., "call to worship," "offertory prayer," "benediction"). Many of these prayers are flexible enough to be used in other times and places. This section also has sacramental resources for Baptism and Holy Communion from The United Methodist Book of Worship and elsewhere.

Part Three: Worship Any Time or Place | These resources are useful—even essential—for a variety of days, in a wide range of settings, with a diversity of people and circumstances. They are organized thematically in the Table of Contents (i.e., "interpersonal prayers," "family and home," "justice and peace," etc.). Many of these prayers could fit within two or more themes; therefore, let the thematic categories be a guide.

Liturgical Leader | Some resources are grouped under the subheading "Resources for Pastors," while the majority are labeled "Resources for All Ministers." The pastoral resources are intended for those who are called and set apart for particular pastoral roles in the Church. Please consult with a denominational body regarding authorization to preside at particular services or components (especially for Baptism and Holy Communion). Items categorized "Resources for All Ministers" may be utilized by all of God's people, lay and clergy.

Resource Types | In this collection, resources labeled "Service" are complete services of worship, whereas resources labeled "Order" are typically embedded within the basic pattern of worship. Resources labeled "litany," "collect," "prayer," or "blessing" are standalone prayers. All sacramental resources are listed under "Resources for Pastors" in Parts Two and Three.

Adaptability | This collection assumes that in a given situation, only the liturgical leader or the one praying will have this book. As such, the majority of resources are written univocally (one voice). However, most can be adapted in a responsive or multivocal style. Additionally, resources written for corporate prayer and resources written for personal prayer can be adapted for either purpose.

When adapting, be sure to plan ahead when possible and to consider the setting. For congregational use—whether adapting from univocal to multivocal or from personal to corporate—practice reading the prayer text aloud. Phrases should be short and words not overly complex, so that the prayer will flow smoothly. See the following examples.

Example: Adapting from univocal to multivocal (the bolded words indicate a communal response)

Univocal	*Multivocal*
Powerful God, we praise you	Powerful God, we praise you
for Jesus Christ,	for Jesus Christ,
who entered the ancient gates in peace,	**who entered the ancient gates in peace,**
whose glory was shown on the cross,	whose glory was shown on the cross,
whose power was shown in love.	**whose power was shown in love.**
We come before you,	We come before you,
not with pure hearts,	not with pure hearts,
not with clean hands,	not with clean hands,
yet we seek your blessing;	**yet we seek your blessing;**
we seek your face.	**we seek your face.**
Grant us your grace and your peace.	Grant us your grace and your peace.
Glory be to you, O God! Amen.	**Glory be to you, O God! Amen.**

Example: Adapting from personal to corporate

Personal	Corporate
Lord, I commit my failures	Lord, we commit our failures
as well as my successes	as well as our successes
into your hands,	into your hands,
and I bring for your healing	and we bring for your healing
the people and the situations,	the people and the situations,
the wrongs and the hurts of the past.	the wrongs and the hurts of the past.
Give me courage, strength and	Give us courage, strength and
generosity	generosity
to let go and move on,	to let go and move on,
leaving the past behind me,	leaving the past behind us,
and living the present to the full.	and living the present to the full.
Lead me always to be positive	Lead us always to be positive
as I entrust the past to your mercy,	as we entrust the past to your mercy,
the present to your love,	the present to your love,
and the future to your providence.	and the future to your providence.

Worship Any Time or Place has been carefully designed for the myriad ways we might use our words and ritual actions to love God and neighbor. May the words and blessings contained within this book be to you, and to all who encounter them, a means of grace. Receive these words of commissioning and blessing from 1 Peter 4:10-11 (NRSVUE):

Like good stewards of the manifold grace of God,
serve one another with whatever gift each of you has received.
Whoever speaks must do so as one speaking the very words of God;
whoever serves must do so with the strength that God supplies,
so that God may be glorified in all things through Jesus Christ.
To him belong the glory and the power for ever and ever.
Amen.

PART ONE

Structures and Seasons

THE BASIC PATTERN
OF WORSHIP

Introduction

The Basic Pattern of Worship is rooted in Scripture and in the heritage and experience of the people called Methodists. It expresses the biblical, historical, and theological integrity of Christian worship and is the basis of all the General Services of the Church. This Basic Pattern is not an order of worship; however, a variety of orders of worship may be based upon it. It reveals that behind the diversity of worship forms and expressions, there is a basic unity.

ENTRANCE

The people come together in the Lord's name. There may be greetings, music and song, prayer and praise.

PROCLAMATION AND RESPONSE

The Scriptures are opened to the people through the reading of lessons, preaching, witnessing, music, or other arts and media. Interspersed may be psalms, anthems, and hymns. Responses to God's Word include acts of commitment and faith with offerings of concerns, prayers, gifts, and service for the world and for one another.

THANKSGIVING AND COMMUNION

In services with Communion, the actions of Jesus in the Upper Room are reenacted:
taking the bread and cup,
giving thanks over the bread and cup,
breaking the bread, and
giving the bread and cup.
In services without Communion, thanks are given for God's mighty acts in Jesus Christ.

SENDING FORTH

The people are sent into ministry with the Lord's blessing.
The United Methodist Book of Worship, adapted

THE RHYTHMS
OF WORSHIP:
THE CHRISTIAN YEAR

The Christian Year, also called the Liturgical Year, is an invitation to participate in a calendrical rhythm that is different from the schedules of our native cultures and competing demands. Visually, the year is often depicted in a circle or spiral, signaling to us the cyclical, dynamic nature of God's timing. Throughout the Christian year, there are two central cycles focused on major events in the life of Christ: the Christmas cycle (Advent-Christmas-Epiphany) and Easter cycle (Lent-Easter-Pentecost). Each of these cycles begins with a time of preparation and anticipation followed by a time of celebration. A season designated as Ordinary Time then follows. The word *ordinary* here does not mean "routine" or "not special." Instead, it refers to the "ordinal numbers" (first, second, third, etc.) used to name and count the Sundays (such as the Third Sunday after Epiphany). Each segment of the Christian Year is imbued with biblical, historical, and theological meanings that connect us with Christians of all denominations and traditions across millennia.

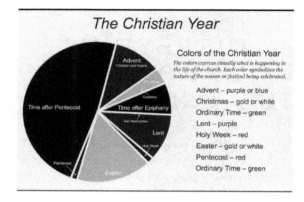

The Christian Year

Colors of the Christian Year

The colors express visually what is happening in the life of the church. Each color symbolizes the nature of the season or festival being celebrated.

Advent – purple or blue
Christmas – gold or white
Ordinary Time – green
Lent – purple
Holy Week – red
Easter – gold or white
Pentecost – red
Ordinary Time – green

Advent

Observances: First Sunday of Advent to the Fourth Sunday of Advent

Color(s): Purple or Blue

Description: The liturgical year begins with Advent, a season of four weeks including four Sundays. *Advent* derives from the Latin *adventus,* which means "coming." In Advent, we proclaim the comings of Christ—preparing for his birth, recognizing his continual presence, and anticipating his final victory. Historically, the season was marked by fasts for preparation. Each Sunday of Advent has a distinct scriptural theme: Christ's coming in final victory (First Sunday), John the Baptist (Second and Third Sundays), and the events immediately preceding the birth of Jesus Christ (Fourth Sunday). The themes of "hope, peace, joy, love" are also used to mark the weeks, but it must be noted that these are creations of worship publishing houses.

Christmas Season

Observances: Nativity of the Lord (Christmas Eve, Christmas Day), First Sunday after Christmas Day, New Year's Eve or New Year's Day, Epiphany of the Lord

Color(s): White or Gold

Description: Christmas is a season of praise and thanksgiving for the incarnation of God in Jesus Christ, which begins with Christmas Eve (December 24 after sundown) or Day and continues through the Day of Epiphany. The name Christmas comes from the season's first service, the Christ Mass. Epiphany comes from the Greek word *epiphania*, which means "manifestation." New Year's Eve or Day is often celebrated in the United Methodist tradition with a Covenant Renewal Service.

Season after the Epiphany

Observances: First Sunday after the Epiphany, Second Sunday after the Epiphany to the Eighth Sunday after the Epiphany, Last Sunday after the Epiphany

Color(s): White (Baptism of the Lord); Green (Second Sunday to the Eighth Sunday after the Epiphany); White (Transfiguration Sunday)

Description: The Season after the Epiphany is a season of Ordinary Time, which includes four to nine Sundays, depending on the date of Easter. It is called "ordinary" because its Sundays are given ordinal numbers (first, second, third, etc.) after the Feast of Epiphany (January 6). It stands between the two great cycles of Advent-Christmas-Epiphany and Lent-Easter-Pentecost. Its central theme is the calling of disciples and the early ministry of Jesus. The First Sunday focuses on the Baptism of Christ and the Last Sunday on the Transfiguration.

Lent

Observances: Ash Wednesday, First Sunday in Lent to the Fifth Sunday in Lent, Sixth Sunday in Lent (Passion/Palm Sunday), Monday through Wednesday of Holy Week, Triduum (Holy Thursday, Good Friday, Holy Saturday)

Color(s): Purple (Ash Wednesday through the Sixth Sunday in Lent); Purple or Red (Monday through Thursday of Holy Week); No Color (Good Friday and Holy Saturday)

Description: "Lent" (from the Anglo-Saxon word *lencten*—referring to the lengthening days of Spring) is a season of forty days, not counting Sundays, which begins on Ash Wednesday and ends on Holy Saturday. Historically, Lent began as a period of fasting and preparation for baptism by converts and then became a time for penance by all Christians. Lent is a time to prepare for the celebration of Easter and invites us to a more somber time of self-reflection and an honest accounting of the ways we have fallen short in our faithful following of the ways of Jesus. However, because we are still an "Easter people," we engage this season always with a recognition of God's grace and an attitude of hope. Holy Week is the final week of Lent, beginning with Passion/Palm Sunday and concluding with Holy Saturday. The Great Three Days—sometimes called the Triduum or Pasch—from sunset Holy Thursday through sunset Easter Day are the climax of Lent (and of the whole Christian year) and a bridge into the Easter Season. These days proclaim the paschal mystery of Jesus Christ's passion, death, and resurrection. During these days, the community journeys with Jesus from the upper room, to the cross, to the tomb, and to the garden.

Easter Season

Observances: Resurrection of the Lord (Easter Eve, Easter Day, Easter Evening), Second Sunday of Easter to the Sixth Sunday of Easter, Ascension of the Lord, Seventh Sunday of Easter, Day of Pentecost

Colors: White or Gold (All Sundays of Easter, Ascension of the Lord); Red (Day of Pentecost)

Description: The Easter Season, also known as the Great Fifty Days, begins at sunset Easter Eve and continues through the Day of Pentecost. It is the most joyous and celebrative season of the Christian year. It focuses on Christ's resurrection and ascension and on the givings of the Holy Spirit on the first Easter (John 20:22-23) and the Day of Pentecost (Acts 2). The ancient Christian name for this festival is *Pasch,* derived from the Hebrew *pesah* ("deliverance" or "passover"), thus connecting the Resurrection to the Exodus. The origin of the English word *Easter* is disputed but may come from the Anglo-Saxon spring goddess *Eastre* and her festival. Pentecost comes from the Greek *pentekoste*, which means "fiftieth." It refers to the Jewish Feast of Weeks, which Greek-speaking Jews called the Day of Pentecost (Acts 2:1). Early Christians also used the term "Pentecost" to refer to the Great Fifty Days as a season. Baptisms, confirmations, and congregational reaffirmation of the Baptismal Covenant are highly appropriate throughout this season, most especially at the First Service of Easter and on the Day of Pentecost.

Season after Pentecost or Ordinary Time

Observances: Trinity Sunday, Sundays after Pentecost (First through Christ the King/Reign of Christ Sunday), All Saints Day, Thanksgiving

Colors: White (Trinity Sunday); Green (Second Sunday after Pentecost to the Twenty-sixth Sunday after Pentecost); White (All Saints); White or Red (Thanksgiving); White (Last Sunday after Pentecost: Christ the King/Reign of Christ Sunday)

Description: The Season after Pentecost, also called Ordinary Time, begins the day after Pentecost and ends the day before the First Sunday of Advent. It may include twenty-three to twenty-eight Sundays, depending on the date of Easter, but the first Sunday is always Trinity Sunday, and the last Sunday is always the Sunday of the Reign of Christ or Christ the King. The season also includes All Saints and Thanksgiving. The purpose of this season is to support new disciples and the whole congregation in living out the gifts and callings discerned during the Easter Season and commissioned on the Day of Pentecost.

The United Methodist Book of Worship
and United Methodist Communications, adapted

PRAYING IN THE STYLE OF A COLLECT

The collect (pronounced "KAW-lekt") is an ancient pattern of prayer with rich content that is short and to the point. Those who learn to pray in this form can quickly and easily compose appropriate prayers for all kinds of occasions. The collect begins with (1) an address to God, utilizing a scriptural, historical, and/or metaphorical name for God. It then (2) articulates attributions of God or acts on which this prayer is based. The prayer then (3) includes a petition (or series of petitions) with (4) rationale or intended outcome(s). It concludes with a (5) doxology that is congruent with the beginning address. The structure of this prayer may be simplified as You, Who, Do, (so that), Through. These are the elements of a collect, as illustrated by the traditional Collect for Purity:

1. Address to God	Almighty God,
2. God's attribute or acts on which this prayer is based	unto whom all hearts are open, all desires known, and from whom no secrets are hid:
3. The petition itself	Cleanse the thoughts of our hearts by the inspiration of thy Holy Spirit,
4. Intended result of the petition	that we may perfectly love thee, and worthily magnify thy holy name;
5. Final doxology	through Christ our Lord. Amen.

The United Methodist Book of Worship, adapted

Part Two

Worship on the Lord's Day

*Resources one would principally use
in the context of a Sunday morning
worship service.*

RESOURCES FOR PASTORS

Baptism

The Baptismal Covenant II-A: A Brief Order of Holy Baptism for Children and Others Unable to Answer for Themselves

This service is designed for situations when the persons baptized are (1) children who cannot take their own vows or (2) youths or adults who have not reached the developmental stage of making decisions for themselves. It is not designed for the baptism of persons who take their own vows, or for confirmation or reaffirmation of faith.

INTRODUCTION OF THE SERVICE AND PRESENTATION OF CANDIDATE(S)

RENUNCIATION OF SIN AND PROFESSION OF FAITH

The pastor addresses parents or other sponsors:

On behalf of the whole Church, I ask you:
Do you reject all that is evil, repent of your sin, and accept the freedom and power God gives you to resist evil, injustice, and oppression in whatever forms they present themselves?
I do.

Do you confess Jesus Christ as your Savior, put your whole
trust in his grace, and promise to serve him as your Lord, in
union with the Church which Christ has opened to people
of all ages, nations, and races?
I do.
Will you nurture these children (persons) in Christ's holy
Church, that by your teaching and example they may be
guided to accept God's grace for themselves, to profess their
faith openly, and to lead a Christian life?
I will.

*The pastor addresses the congregation, and the congregation
responds:*

Do you, as Christ's body, the Church, reaffirm both your
rejection of sin and your commitment to Christ?
We do.
Will you nurture one another in the Christian faith and life,
include these persons now before you in your care, and surround them with a community of love and forgiveness?
We will.

THANKSGIVING OVER THE WATER

Eternal Father, your mighty acts of salvation
have been made known through water—
from the moving of your Spirit upon the waters of creation,
to the deliverance of your people
through the flood and through the Red Sea.
In the fullness of time you sent Jesus,
nurtured in the water of a womb, baptized by John,
and anointed by your Spirit.
He called his disciples
to share in the baptism of his death and resurrection
and to make disciples of all nations.

Pour out your Holy Spirit,
to bless this gift of water and those who receive it,
to wash away their sin and clothe them in righteousness
throughout their lives
that, dying and being raised with Christ,
they may share in his final victory;
through the same Jesus Christ our Lord. **Amen.**

BAPTISM WITH LAYING ON OF HANDS

As each candidate is baptized, the pastor uses the Christian name(s), but not the surname:

Christian Name(s), I baptize you in the name of the Father,
and of the Son,
and of the Holy Spirit. **Amen.**

Immediately after the administration of the water, the pastor places hands on the candidate's head and invokes the work of the Holy Spirit. Other persons, including baptized members of the candidate's family, may join the pastor in this action. During the laying on of hands, the pastor says:

The Holy Spirit work within you,
that being born through water and the Spirit,
you may be a faithful disciple of Jesus Christ. **Amen.**

COMMENDATION AND WELCOME

The pastor addresses the congregation:

Members of the household of God, I commend these persons to your love and care. Will you do all in your power to increase their faith, confirm their hope, and perfect them in love?
We will.

As members in the body of Christ and in this congregation of The United Methodist Church, will you renew your covenant faithfully to participate in the ministries of the church by your prayers, your presence, your gifts, your service, and your witness that in everything God may be glorified through Jesus Christ?
We will.

The pastor addresses those baptized and their parents and sponsors:

The God of all grace,
who has called us to eternal glory in Christ,
establish you and strengthen you
by the power of the Holy Spirit,
that you may live in grace and peace.

One or more laypersons, including children, may join the pastor in acts of welcome and peace. Baptized children may be welcomed by a kiss of peace or other acts or words immediately following Baptism with Laying on of Hands. Then an appropriate hymn, stanza, or response may be sung. Appropriate thanksgivings and intercessions for those who have participated in these acts should be included in the Concerns and Prayers that follow. It is most fitting that the service continue with Holy Communion, in which the union of the newly baptized children with the body of Christ is most fully expressed.
The United Methodist Book of Worship, adapted

A Celebration of a Renewed Believer through Testimony and Baptismal Reaffirmation

INTRODUCTION

The person making a public profession of faith and a reaffirmation of the baptismal covenant is invited to stand before the congregation (or another arrangement they have made with the pastor and/or the worship leadership team).

People of God, co-heirs with Christ:
through the sacrament of baptism
God's Spirit has been poured out upon water,
water poured over and immersing us,
water that flows freely for all who will receive it,
water from the streams of God's saving power and justice,
water that brings hope to all who thirst for righteousness,
water that refreshes life, nurtures growth,
and offers new birth.

Today we come to the waters,
to celebrate *N.*'s faith in the presence of this assembly.
We also come to the waters to celebrate our recommitment
to Christ who has raised us,
to the Spirit who has birthed us,
and to the Creator who is making all things new.

TESTIMONY

We have asked *N.* to share with us how God has been at work by offering his/her/their testimony. Let us be attentive in this holy moment.

Testimony is offered by the renewed believer.

Appropriate transitional words are offered, leading to the re-nunciation of sin and profession of faith.

RENUNCIATION OF SIN AND PROFESSION
OF FAITH

To the renewed believer:

And so I ask you, will you turn away from the powers of sin and death and repent of your sin?
If so, say, "I will."
I will.

Will you let the Spirit use you as a prophetic witness to the powers that be, resisting evil, injustice, and oppression in whatever forms they present themselves?
If so, say, "I will."
I will.

Will you proclaim the good news, confessing Jesus Christ as your savior, putting your trust in his grace, living as his disciple?
If so, say, "I will."
I will.

Will you be a living witness to the gospel wherever you are, and in all that you do?
If so, say, "I will."
I will.

Will you receive and profess the Christian faith as contained in the scriptures of the Old and New Testaments?
If so, say, "I will."
I will.

To the assembly:
To all of us gathered, will you also turn from sin, resist evil, proclaim the good news, and serve as a witness to Christ in this world, grounded in our faith handed down through the holy scriptures?
If so, say, "We will."
We will.

THANKSGIVING OVER THE WATER

Let us pray.
Almighty God, we give you thanks for the new life
you birthed in us by water and the Holy Spirit,
for the washing away of our sins,
for incorporating us into the church universal
and for calling us to live in holy imitation of Christ.

We confess that we have not always
held up our end of the covenant.
We have neglected the living water.
We have parched ourselves, and we are dry and thirsty, O God.
Refresh us today.

Come, Holy Spirit!
Come upon these waters.
Let these waters remind us of the grace
declared to us in our baptism.
Let these waters be to us drops of your mercy,
couriers of your faithfulness.
Let these waters renew in us
the resurrection power of Jesus.
Let these waters make us long for
and participate in your coming reign.

Glory to you, God the Father [and Mother] of us all!
Glory to you, God the Son, our Lord Jesus Christ!
Glory to you, God the Spirit, our guide and companion!

Eternal God, One in Three and Three in One!
All glory is yours, now and forever. Amen!

INDIVIDUAL BAPTISMAL REMEMBRANCE

In this moment, it may be appropriate to invite the congregation to stand and extend their hands toward the one remembering their baptism as an act of support.

Pastor says to renewed believer:

N., we celebrate the transformative power of God—Father, Son, and Holy Spirit—in your life. You have offered your testimony and you have professed your faith in the presence of this assembly of faith.

Pastor dips hand in the water, then while making the sign of the cross on the believer's forehead, says:

N., as a public witness to God's mighty acts in your life,
Remember that you are baptized, and rejoice!

Optional communal response:
Remember that you are baptized, and rejoice!

Friends, let us give thanks for *N.'s* public profession of faith
and remembrance of baptism.
Allow time for acts of celebration and gratitude, such as applause.
Thanks be to God.
Amen.

COMMUNAL BAPTISMAL REMEMBRANCE

*At this time, the pastor may invite the renewed believer to assist
in helping the rest of the assembly remember their baptisms.
Hymns of praise should accompany this joyous remembrance.*

> The United Methodist Book of Worship
> Discipleship Ministries
> Nelson Cowan

A Prayer Following Remembrance of Baptism

Deep, flowing mystery of God,
gentle, life-giving grace of God,
we immerse ourselves in you.
We descend into your watery embrace,
baptized in your blessing.
With Jesus, we know your delight in us,
we trust your Spirit in us,
and we hear your calling.
By your summons, we rise,
we follow, and we serve you,
in the living, breathing spirit of Christ. Amen.

> *Steve Garnaas-Holmes*

Holy Communion

An Alternative Great Thanksgiving for General Use

The pastor stands behind the Lord's table.

The Lord be with you.
And also with you.
Lift up your hearts.

The pastor may lift hands and keep them raised.
We lift them up to the Lord.
Let us give thanks to the Lord our God.
It is right to give our thanks and praise.

Blessed are you, our Alpha and our Omega,
whose strong and loving arms encompass the universe,
for with your eternal Word and Holy Spirit
you are forever one God.
Through your Word you created all things
and called them good,
and in you we live and move and have our being.
When we fell into sin, you did not desert us.
You made covenant with your people Israel
and spoke through prophets and teachers.
In Jesus Christ your Word became flesh and dwelt among us,
full of grace and truth.

And so, with your people on earth
and all the company of heaven
we praise your name and join their unending hymn:

The pastor may lower hands.

**Holy, holy, holy Lord, God of power and might,
heaven and earth are full of your glory.**

Hosanna in the highest.
Blessed is he who comes in the name of the Lord.
Hosanna in the highest.

The pastor may raise hands.

Holy are you, and blessed is Jesus Christ,
who called you Abba, Father.
As a mother tenderly gathers her children,
you embraced a people as your own
and filled them with a longing for a peace that would last
and for a justice that would never fail.
In Jesus' suffering and death you took upon yourself
our sin and death
and destroyed their power for ever.
You raised from the dead this same Jesus,
who now reigns with you in glory,
and poured upon us your Holy Spirit,
making us the people of your new covenant.

*The pastor may hold hands, palms down, over the bread, or
touch the bread, or lift the bread.*

On the night before meeting with death, Jesus took bread,
gave thanks to you, broke the bread, gave it to the disciples,
and said:
"Take, eat; this is my body which is given for you.
Do this in remembrance of me."

*The pastor may hold hands, palms down, over the cup, or
touch the cup, or lift the cup.*

When the supper was over Jesus took the cup,
gave thanks to you, gave it to the disciples, and said:
"Drink from this, all of you;
this is my blood of the new covenant,

poured out for you and for many for the forgiveness of sins.
Do this, as often as you drink it, in remembrance of me."

The pastor may raise hands.

And so, in remembrance of these
your mighty acts in Jesus Christ,
we offer ourselves in praise and thanksgiving
as a holy and living sacrifice,
in union with Christ's offering for us,
as we proclaim the mystery of faith.

Christ has died; Christ is risen; Christ will come again.

The pastor may hold hands, palms down, over the bread and cup.

Pour out your Holy Spirit on us gathered here,
and on these gifts,
that in the breaking of this bread
and the drinking of this wine
we may know the presence of the living Christ
and be renewed as the body of Christ for the world,
redeemed by Christ's blood.

The pastor may raise hands.

As the grain and grapes, once dispersed in the fields,
are now united on this table in bread and wine,
so may we and all your people be gathered
from every time and place
into the unity of your eternal household
and feast at your table for ever.

Through Christ, with Christ, in Christ,
in the unity of the Holy Spirit,
all honor and glory is yours, almighty God, now and forever.

Amen.

The United Methodist Book of Worship

A Concise Great Thanksgiving for General Use

Let us pray.

We orient our hearts to you and give you thanks,
Almighty God.
Through your divine creativity, you spoke the universe,
the heavens,
and our world into existence.
You fashioned us in your image, loving and relational.
When we strayed from your goodness and our love faltered,
your love remained faithful.

Through the birth, life, death, and resurrection
of your Son Jesus Christ
you destroyed the power of sin and death forever,
and made with us a new covenant by water and the Spirit.
With gratitude, our hearts echo the song of heaven,
declaring your holiness and blessedness from age to age.

We remember the night Jesus delivered Himself up
for the life and salvation of the world,
how he took bread, gave thanks to you, broke the bread,
shared it with his disciples, and said:
"Take, eat; this is my body which is given for you.
Do this in remembrance of me."
When the supper was over,
we remember how he took the cup,
gave thanks to you, shared it with his disciples, and said:
"Drink from this, all of you;
this is my blood of the new covenant,
poured out for you and for many for the forgiveness of sins.

Do this, as often as you drink it, in remembrance of me."

Remembering these liberating acts of Jesus Christ,
we offer ourselves in praise and thanksgiving
as a holy and living sacrifice,
in union with Christ's offering for us.

Pour out your Holy Spirit on us gathered here,
and on these gifts,
that in the breaking of this bread and the drinking of this cup
we may know the living Christ
and be nourished as His body, for the sake of the world,
until that glorious day when love's redeeming work is done,
on earth as it is in heaven.

We bless you, Almighty God, Trinity of love;
one God, now and forever. Amen.

The United Methodist Book of Worship
Nelson Cowan

An Intergenerational Great Thanksgiving

Inspired by Jewish Table Prayers

*This prayer may be prayed univocally or in litany form. If praying
as a litany, you'll want the repeated phrase to be the opening line
"Blessed are you, Lord our God." Consider cueing people with a
hand gesture or a vocal cue (or both) to encourage participation.*

Blessed are you, Lord our God,
Creator of all.
From the rising of the sun to its setting,
your name is praised among all peoples.
In the power of your Word and Holy Spirit,
you created all things, blessed them, and called them good.

You called us to be your people, but we did not answer.
You were faithful, but we wandered from the way.
Still, you called us to return, and led us home.

Blessed are you, Lord our God,
who came and dwelt among us, as one of us, in Jesus
Christ:
bringing good news to the poor,
healing the sick, raising the dead,
sharing table with the unrighteous,
and teaching the way that leads to life.

Blessed are you, Lord our God,
who brings forth bread from the earth.
The night before he died,
Jesus broke bread and shared it with these words:
"Take, eat; this is my body which is given for you.
Do this in remembrance of me."

Blessed are you, Lord our God,
who creates the fruit of the vine.
Jesus shared the cup with these words:
"Drink from this, all of you;
this is my blood of the new covenant,
poured out for the forgiveness of sin.
Do this in remembrance of me."

Blessed are you, Lord our God,
present with us as the Holy Spirit.
We remember the story of your love for us
with praise and thanksgiving!
Pour out your Holy Spirit on each of us and on these gifts.
May they become the body and the blood of Christ,
so we may become the love of Christ in this world.

Blessed are you, Lord our God,
Father, Son, Holy Spirit;
with you and with all your children past, present, and
future,
we give you praise now and forever.
Amen.

Michelle L. Whitlock

RESOURCES FOR ALL MINISTERS

Words for Gathering

A.

The Lord be with you
And also with you
Receive these words of invitation:
No matter what you have done, or left undone;
no matter who you love, or who you have failed to love;
whether you are here to be joyful;
whether you are here to mourn;
whether you are here and you are still figuring out
the beauty and messiness of faith;
our God welcomes us in this place.
All are welcome in this place.
Amen.

Nelson Cowan

B.

If you are spiritually weary and in search of rest,
if you are mourning and you long for comfort,
if you are struggling and you desire victory,
if you recognize that you are a sinner and need a Savior,
God welcomes you here in the name of Christ.
To the stranger in need of fellowship,
to those who hunger and thirst for righteousness,
and to whoever will come,
this congregation opens wide its doors
and welcomes all in the name of the Lord Jesus Christ.

Reformed Worship

C.
This is the day that the LORD has made;
let us rejoice and be glad in it.

Psalm 118:24 NRSVUE

D.
Come!
Come into the place where God listens!
Where you need no money, no status, no fine clothes!
Come as you are
Broken, whole
Sick, well
Satisfied or with deep needs
Come to sing
Come to cry
Come to hear
Come to see
Come and be ready or come to be made ready
We are here
God is here too

Liturgies from Below

E.
Sometimes worship is a parade, a celebration,
a gathering of people expressing their joy.
Sometimes worship is an adventure, a quest,
a gathering of people searching for meaning.
Sometimes worship is a funeral, a fast,
a gathering of people seeking comfort in their grief.
Among us today are people who have come to march, people
who have come to search, people who have come to weep
. . . yet we have all come to acknowledge God and to touch
each other.
Come with open minds, open hearts, open arms;
that we all might find that for which we have come
and that, as well, we all might be surprised.

John W. Howell

F.
Jesus said, "Follow me."
We don't always know what that means.
We are on a journey of discovery. We are here because we want to be God's people; we are here because we are broken and want to be whole again; we are here to celebrate our lives, and God's presence in this life. Let us worship God with great thanks giving.

M. Enid Watson

G.
The Lord be with you.
And also with you.
God has gathered us here today,
a day in which we bring our full selves—
our simplicity, our complexity,
our joy, our sadness,
our vigilance, our apathy,
our hopes, our fears.
In the midst of our own stories,
we gather here to be found in God's story—
a God who welcomes all people,
a God who loves all people without conditions,
and beyond measure.
So let us gather, and let us worship.
Amen.

Nelson Cowan

H.
Receive these words of invitation:
God has created the world and called it "good."
God has created each of us in God's image
and called us "good."

The rocks cry out to the living God.
The mountains bow down before God.
The rivers and streams proclaim God's handiwork.
And it is *this* God who welcomes us today—
who meets us where we are,
and proclaims that we are God's beloved.
Let us sing, rejoice, rest, and be glad
in that profound identity today.
Amen.

Nelson Cowan

Opening Prayers / Invocations

A.
Almighty God,
to you all hearts are open, all desires known,
and from you no secrets are hidden.
Cleanse the thoughts of our hearts
by the inspiration of your Holy Spirit,
that we may perfectly love you,
and worthily magnify your holy name,
through Christ our Lord. Amen.

The Collect for Purity

B.
Sing to the Lord, all the earth!
Share the news of God's saving work every single day!
Declare God's glory among the nations;
declare God's wondrous works among all people
because the Lord is great and so worthy of praise.

1 Chronicles 16:23-25, alt.

C.

Almighty God, through your only Son you overcame death
and opened to us the gate of everlasting life.
Grant that we who celebrate our Lord's resurrection,
by the renewing of your Spirit,
arise from the death of sin to the life of righteousness;
through the same Jesus Christ our Lord. Amen.

Gelasian Sacramentary

D.

New every morning is your love, great God of light,
and all day long you are working for good in the world.
Stir up in us desire to serve you,
to live peacefully with our neighbors,
and to devote each day to your Son, our Savior, Jesus Christ
the Lord. Amen.

Presbyterian Worshipbook

E.

Thanks be to you, O God, author of eternal light.
Continually shine forth upon us who watch for you,
that our lips may praise you, our lives bless you,
and our meditation glorify you;
through Jesus Christ, the Light of the world we pray. Amen.

Sarum Breviary, alt.

F.

God of grace,
you have given us minds to know you, hearts to love you,
and voices to sing your praise.
Fill us with your Spirit, that we may celebrate your glory
and worship you in spirit and in truth;
through Jesus Christ, our Lord. Amen.

The Worship Sourcebook

G.

Light of God, illumine the path that leads us to healing,
hope, and salvation.
Glory of God, fill this sanctuary
and expose the darkness that stalks our souls.
Light of God, shine with such brightness
that we marvel in awe.
Glory of God, fill each temple of the Holy Spirit present to-
day.
Light of God, Glory of God, we welcome you in this place.
Amen.

Kwasi I. Kena

H.

O Lord, how manifold are your works!
In wisdom you have made them all.
Open your hand to us, O God, giver of good things.
Do not hide your face from us.
Should you remove your Spirit from us,
we shall surely return to the dust.
Send forth your Spirit in this worship service today
and let us be re-created.
Renew us, O God, with your Spirit.
In Jesus' name. Amen.

Marilyn E. Thornton

I.

O God, you pour out your spirit of grace and love.
Deliver us from cold hearts and wandering thoughts,
that with burning zeal and steady minds
we may worship you in spirit and truth. Amen.

Ancient Collects and Other Prayers

J.

O God, our Guide and Guardian,
you have led us apart from the busy world
into the quiet of your house.
Grant us grace to worship you in spirit and in truth,
to the comfort of our souls
and the upbuilding of every good purpose and holy desire.
Enable us to do more perfectly the work
to which you have called us,
that we may not fear the coming of night,
when we shall resign into your hands
the tasks which you have committed to us.
So may we worship you not with our lips at this hour,
but in word and deed all the days of our lives;
through Jesus Christ our Savior. Amen.

The Book of Worship 1965, alt.

K.

O Lord our God,
you are always more ready to bestow your good gifts on us
than we are to seek them,
and are willing to give more than we desire or deserve.
Help us so to seek that we may truly find,
so to ask that we may joyfully receive,
so to knock that the door of your mercy may be opened to us;
through Jesus Christ our Savior. Amen.

The Book of Common Prayer, alt.

L.

A text especially mindful of children

Dear God, our friend,
we come to worship you today.
We come to sing, pray, and listen.
You always hear us.
Help us to hear you. Amen.

The Hymnal Project

M.

Hallelujah Hallelujah
Praise be to God
To the God of land
God of the sea
God of the sky
God of the mountains,
The God of rain
The provider of manna
God of our mothers and fathers
Come and be with us this morning
as we bring our hearts to worship you
We come to you with our hearts
that are dry, hopeless and heavy
With hope that you are the God that provides,
You are the God of yesterday, today and tomorrow. Amen.

Liturgies from Below

N.

Gracious God, you loved the world so much,
you gave your only begotten Son,
who lived, died, and rose again
for the sake of the world;
that whoever believes in him
shall not perish, but have eternal life.
Grant us the boldness of this resurrection faith,
that we might be transformed for the sake of the world;
through Jesus Christ our Lord,
in the power of the Holy Spirit.
Amen.

Nelson Cowan

O.

Creator God, as you have gathered us in generations past,
lead and guide us this day
as we seek your wisdom and your vision for our people.
Give us eyes to see one another as you see us,
people of one God,
connected to one another and to you in all our relations,
and in your son Jesus.
Give us ears to hear the wisdom of our elders
and the laughter of our children.
Give us words of blessing and healing for a hurting world.
Open our hearts and lead us on the path of peace.
We stand together on sacred ground with grateful hearts,
knowing that the One who promises is faithful and true.
Amen.

Delana Taylor

P.

One: Love, without it we are like clanging cymbals,
All: Love!
One: We can speak like prophets, but we still have to
All: Love!
One: We can build great buildings, but we need to
All: Love!
One: We can preach and pray, thank God everyday,
but we must
All: Love!
One: Be patient and kind, with no envy in mind,
All: Love!
One: Don't be rude or resentful;
don't insist on your own way,
All: Love!

One: How can we live without it?
All: Love!
One: How can we sing without it?
All: Love!
One: Who can serve God without it?
All: Love!
One: We just stopped by today
so that God could remind us to
All: Love!

Kwasi I. Kenna

Q.

Jesus Christ, Lord of the Church: we rejoice that you have formed your people into one body comprised of believers of every race and nation. Your salvation has reached to the ends of the earth and to all generations. We praise and thank you that your gospel has reached us and that our voices will join those of many languages this day to proclaim your praise. Accept our praise, purify our hearts, instruct us in your word, feed us at your table, and visit us with your Spirit that we may follow in the ways of faith, to the glory of God the Father. Amen.

Constance Cherry

R.

Almighty God,
you have given us grace at this time with one accord to make our common supplication to you; and you have promised through your well-beloved Son that when two or three are gathered together in his name, you will be in the midst of them. Fulfill now, O Lord, our desires and petitions as may be best for us; granting us in this world knowledge of your truth, and in the age to come life everlasting. Amen.

John Chrysostom, alt., The Book of Common Prayer

S.

Powerful God, we praise you for Jesus Christ,
who entered the ancient gates in peace,
whose glory was shown on the cross,
whose power was shown in love.
We come before you,
not with pure hearts,
not with clean hands,
yet we seek your blessing;
we seek your face.
Grant us your grace and your peace.
Glory be to you, O God! Amen.

Ruth Duck

T.

You have broken into our lives, O God,
creating the world anew today.
You have breathed new life into our sleeping souls
and have put a song in our hearts.
So we come today to offer you our thanks and praise.
Pour down the blessings of your Spirit
upon each one here this morning,
that we may perceive your nearness once more.
This we pray in the name of Jesus the Christ. Amen.

James H. Hill

Creeds and Affirmations of Faith

The Nicene Creed

We believe in one God,
the Father, the Almighty,
maker of heaven and earth,
of all that is, seen and unseen.

We believe in one Lord, Jesus Christ,
the only Son of God,
eternally begotten of the Father,
God from God, Light from Light,
true God from true God,
begotten, not made,
of one Being with the Father;
through him all things were made.
For us and for our salvation
he came down from heaven,
was incarnate of the Holy Spirit and the Virgin Mary
and became truly human.
For our sake he was crucified under Pontius Pilate;
he suffered death and was buried.
On the third day he rose again
in accordance with the Scriptures;
he ascended into heaven
and is seated at the right hand of the Father.
He will come again in glory
to judge the living and the dead,
and his kingdom will have no end.
We believe in the Holy Spirit, the Lord, the giver of life,
who proceeds from the Father and the Son,
who with the Father and the Son
is worshiped and glorified,
who has spoken through the prophets.
We believe in one holy catholic* and apostolic church.
We acknowledge one baptism
for the forgiveness of sins.
We look for the resurrection of the dead,
and the life of the world to come. Amen.

*universal

The United Methodist Hymnal

The Apostles' Creed (Traditional Version)

I believe in God, the Father Almighty,
maker of heaven and earth;

And in Jesus Christ his only Son, our Lord;
who was conceived by the Holy Spirit,
born of the Virgin Mary,
suffered under Pontius Pilate,
was crucified, dead, and buried;*
the third day he rose from the dead;
he ascended into heaven,
and sitteth at the right hand of God the Father Almighty;
from thence he shall come to judge the quick and the dead.

I believe in the Holy Spirit,
the holy catholic** church,
the communion of saints,
the forgiveness of sins,
the resurrection of the body,
and the life everlasting. Amen.

*Traditional use of this creed includes these words:
"He descended into hell."

**universal*

The United Methodist Hymnal

The Apostles' Creed (Ecumenical Version)

I believe in God, the Father Almighty,
creator of heaven and earth.

I believe in Jesus Christ, his only Son, our Lord,
who was conceived by the Holy Spirit,
born of the Virgin Mary,

suffered under Pontius Pilate,
was crucified, died, and was buried;
he descended to the dead.
On the third day he rose again;
he ascended into heaven,
is seated at the right hand of the Father,
and will come again to judge the living and the dead.

I believe in the Holy Spirit,
the holy catholic** church,
the communion of saints,
the forgiveness of sins,
the resurrection of the body,
and the life everlasting. Amen.

**universal*

The United Methodist Hymnal

Land Acknowledgments

Land acknowledgments are formal public statements, showing awareness, gratitude, honor, and respect for the first people(s) of particular lands, territories, and spaces. In most places, the effort to create such a statement reveals, reminds, and confronts the authors and audience with the reality, among others, that they are not the first ones here. Someone(s) else was here first. The Indigenous people of most lands have been and/or are being made invisible. The church has benefited greatly.

Land acknowledgments can be a powerful way to subvert forces and systems that benefit from the erasure, genocide, assimilation, and colonization of the original inhabitants. At the same time, if written without any plans for next steps (such as cultivating authentic relationships and/or plans for reparations), land acknowledgments can also function as performative "feel good" allyship, which further perpetuates colonial legacies. Acknowledgment is an important first step toward dismantling racism. It is a way to help make the invisible visible again. This guide is meant to help resource individuals and communities who would like to research, create, and share in the practice of land acknowledgment.

General guidelines for writing a land acknowledgment:

Research. Learn more about the way in which you acquired the land where your site is (this map can help you identify the unceded territory your church occupies: https://native-land.ca/).

Write. Understand that this is a living document and will need some work after you first publish it.

Share. Learn more about the Indigenous people whose land you now reside upon and remember, even though generations have passed, your local Indigenous community still exists.

Follow the Spirit. As you craft your land acknowledgment, be prepared for resistance from others and maybe from yourself. Explore what that is about. Also, consider what more you and your ministry setting can do to create a circle of friendship and healing with your local Indigenous communities.

The Greater Northwest Circle of Indigenous Ministries, adapted

Examples:

A.

Creator, you made all people of every land. It is our responsibility to give thanks and respect to those who first occupied this land we are upon. We give thanks to _____, the first people of this land. We offer our respect to those ancestors who may be interred in this land. We are also thankful for the gifts of the People of the land. Creator, let us be of good mind to reconcile the mistreatment of this land and to those who have been displaced. With thankful and respectful hearts, we pray in Your Name, Your son the Peacemaker and the Sacred Spirit. Amen.

Unknown, Multiple Origins

B.

For thousands of years, the space where we prayerfully gather today was under the care of the *[specify the native people who originally lived where your church is]*. Their presence in this region is remembered and woven into the history of our community. On this Sunday and every day, we are encouraged to partner in repairing past harm and to move forward with awareness and respect, celebrating and embracing the contributions of First Americans.

Liturgy, Native American Ministries Sunday

Prayers for Illumination

A.

Lord, open our hearts and minds
by the power of your Holy Spirit,
that as the Scriptures are read
and your Word proclaimed,
we may hear with joy what you say to us today. Amen.

The United Methodist Book of Worship

B.

God, in Christ Jesus, you appeared to your disciples after
the resurrection—behind closed doors, needing a word from
you. Speak peace to us, now, and let us hear your voice in
the proclamation of your truth. Help our doubt in this hour,
even as you extend the proof of your presence—scarred
hands and a healing heart. Amen.

Valerie Bridgeman Davis

C.

Holy God,
author of the Word made flesh,
to whom belongs both the first Word and the last,
open us to your Spirit,
that as scripture is spoken and your Word proclaimed,
we may be comforted, convinced, and changed
to the glory of Jesus Christ, in whose name we pray. Amen.

Brian Wren

D.

We give thanks, O God of sacred stories, for the witness of
holy scripture. Through it, you nurture our imaginations,

touch our feelings, increase our awareness, and challenge our assumptions. Bless, we pray, our hearing of your word this day. Speak to each of us; speak to all of us; and grant that by the power of your Spirit, we may be hearers and doers of your word. Amen.

Ann B. Day

E.
Mighty God,
through whom we come to know
the love and healing power of Jesus:
By the power of your Holy Spirit open our minds and hearts
that we may hear what you have to say to us today. Amen.

OSL Daily Office IV-B

F.
Speak to us, O God!
Speak to us through song,
through story,
through imagination.
Speak to us through your Spirit.
In the name of Christ, we pray. Amen.

Nelson Cowan

Prayers of Confession

A.
O blessed Spirit of Truth,
you search the heart and test the inmost thoughts,
help me remember my sins,
and let me see them in your light.
Strengthen me also with courage to confess them truly,

hiding nothing, excusing nothing,
keeping back nothing in my heart.
In your mercy, pardon and absolve,
and thus heal me,
that I may arise and sin no more,
through the merits and for the sake
of Jesus Christ, my Lord and only Savior. Amen.

Mozarabic Sacramentary

B.

O Lord, we forget you.
We forget to pray.
When we pray, we forget to thank you.
When we pray, we forget our sisters and brothers.
When we pray, we forget your joy.
When we pray, we forget your good news.
We forget what you've done for us from the first days till now.
O Lord, we forget. Forgive us for being so forgetful.

Tony Peterson

C.

Gracious God,
Though we live in a culture that is reluctant to admit guilt,
assume responsibility, or ask for forgiveness,
we are so bold as to pray the words of the psalmist who said,
Search me, O God, and know my heart;
test me and know my thoughts;
see if there is any wicked way in me,
and lead me in the way everlasting
(Psalm 139:23-24 NRSV).
Search us, O God, and reveal anything in our lives
that stands between us and your love.
Search us, O God, and show us our sins

so that we might confess them.
Search us, O God, and show us places
where we have neglected Christian responsibility,
and then teach us how to live on this earth with each other.
Search us, O God, and show us the faces
of those we have wronged,
so that we might seek their forgiveness.

(Silence)

Words of Assurance: We have not been called to this hour of worship to wallow in sin and self-pity. God has promised to forgive our sins when we confess them and to cleanse us from all manner of unrighteousness (1 John 1:9). Rise from your knees as children of God, forgiven from sin and empowered to lead holy lives.
All: Amen.

Safiyah Fosua

D.

Gracious God,
our sins are too heavy to carry,
too real to hide, and too deep to undo.
Forgive what our lips tremble to name,
what our hearts can no longer bear,
and what has become for us a consuming fire of judgment.
Set us free from a past we cannot change;
open to us a future in which we can be changed;
and grant us grace
to grow more and more in your likeness and image;
through Jesus Christ, the light of the world.

United Church of Christ,
Office for Church Life and Leadership

E.

God of truth,
you have spoken your Word to us and in us
but we have not listened to you.
We have not been mindful of your presence,
or attentive to your voice.
Have mercy on us, forgive us, and heal us.
Speak your Word in us now, and create us anew.
We open ourselves to your Word.

Steve Garnaas-Holmes

F.

Merciful God,
we have not loved you with our whole heart
nor our neighbors as ourselves.
For the sake of your Son Jesus Christ, forgive what we
have been, accept us as we are, and guide what we shall be,
through Jesus Christ our Lord. Amen.

Supplement to the Book of Common Prayer, alt.

G.

God of all mercy,
we confess that we have sinned against you,
opposing your will in our lives.
We have denied your goodness in each other, in ourselves,
and in the world you have created.
We repent of the sins we have done.
We commit ourselves to resist evil, injustice and oppression
in whatever forms they present themselves, especially when
they are done in your name.
We seek your power to deliver us from sins that still beset us.
Forgive, restore, and strengthen us through our Savior Jesus
Christ, that we may abide in your love and always discern
and do your will. Amen.

The Church Pension Fund, alt. Taylor Burton-Edwards

Pastoral Prayers and Intercessions

A. A Prayer for Peace and Justice (John 3:17)

God, we pray for our troubled world.
We thank you that you labor to renew creation,
that you seek not to judge but to save,
not to destroy but to create.
We praise you that you call the nations to peace,
and the peoples to justice.
With you we mourn that children around the world
still fall in war's violence,
and that many children become homeless, hungry,
and thirsty in the wake of war.
We pray for people everywhere
who struggle for freedom
before those who rule through terror,
who plunder the poor and imprison the just.
Save us, O God, from helplessness.
Speak to us and show us each our part to play
in your mission of saving the world through your love.
Cleanse us from all that keeps us from serving you
and loving our neighbors in integrity of word and deed.
We pray to you in the strong name of Jesus Christ. Amen.

Ruth Duck

B. Prayer of Intercession: Losing, Seeking, Finding (Luke 15)

God of the lost,
like travelers without a map
we have sometimes taken wrong turns in life.
Like children in a crowd separated from their parents,
we become afraid
and long with all our being for a familiar, beloved voice.

We pray now for all who are seeking direction,
who need to start over, who are lonely and fearful.

[Silence]

God of the forgotten,
we bring to mind those who have asked for our prayers
and others we do not know for whom you call us to pray.

[Silence]

God of welcome and of love,
who weeps with those who weep
and rejoices with those who rejoice,
we thank you for seeking all who have lost their way,
for you guide them toward the path of life,
and you show the way from estrangement to reunion.
We shout with joy for those who are coming home
to restored relationship with you and your people.

[Silence]

And now, Holy One,
we pray you to search out the places in each of us
that remain lost from you and the power of your love.
Seek us, find us, that like Jesus Christ
we and our communities of faith
may be havens of home to all people,
for it is in the name of Jesus we pray. Amen.

Ruth Duck

C.
The Holy One be with you.
And also with you.
Let us pray.

Beginning and End of all things,
we bless you for the present that is ever yielding

to your new heaven and new earth.
We offer you our praise for all the means of grace
and for every prompting of your Spirit,
calling us to spurn sin and open ourselves
to your presence and purpose.
Merciful God,
Hear our prayer.

Here members of the community are invited to lift up thanks-givings and concerns, concluding each petition with "Merciful God," to which the community responds:

"Hear our prayer."

We yield our concerns to your unceasing mercy:
care for the sick and the suffering,
touch the dying,
claim the newborn,
shelter the homeless,
sing in the faithful,
chasten the arrogant and powerful,
lift up the lowly,
center the Church,
grant peace to every people,
and shape our lives by the mystery of Christ.
Merciful God,
Hear our prayer.
Amen.

Dan Benedict

D. Send a Healing Word (Lamentations 3:19-26)
One Voice: We have entered this sacred space, broken, hurt-ing, seeking, numb from the cares of the world that weigh us down.
Many Voices: Send a healing word to us today, O Lord.

One Voice: We have come from near and far, from various backgrounds, strangers yet connected in and through you.
Many Voices: Send a healing word to us today, O Lord.
One Voice: We long to draw closer to you; we need to draw closer to one another.
Many Voices: Send a healing word to us today, O Lord.
One Voice: Send a word from on high that will comfort, enlighten, enliven, and inspire us this day.
Many Voices: Send a healing word to us today, O Lord.
One Voice: Then bind us together as daughters and sisters, sons and brothers, family in the faith that we might speak words of comfort, healing, wisdom, and love as witnesses to the amazing Mother, Father, Friend, Confidante we have found in our relationship with you, Lord.
Many Voices: Send a healing word to us today, O Lord.

Sharletta M. Green

E.
We strip ourselves of the desire to live according to our will.
Clothe us in the Holy Spirit.
We strip ourselves of doubts and fears.
Clothe us in the Holy Spirit.
We strip ourselves of the oppression and hatred that attempt to hold us.
Clothe us in the Holy Spirit.
We strip ourselves of bitterness, frustration, and anger.
Clothe us in the Holy Spirit.
We strip ourselves of the stubbornness that keeps us from moving where you have commanded us to go.
Clothe us in the Holy Spirit.
We strip ourselves of the evil that calls to us daily.
Clothe us in the Holy Spirit.
We strip ourselves of the complacency that keeps us from truly being your disciples.

Clothe us in the Holy Spirit.
With all that calls to us, Lord, we are weakened when we
dress ourselves in the ways of this world. Our strength comes
from you alone.
Clothe us in the Holy Spirit.

Ciona Rouse

F.
Let us pray for the Church and for the world.
Grant, almighty God,
that all who confess your name may be united in your truth,
live together in your love, and reveal your glory in the world.
Lord, in your mercy, **hear our prayer**. *Silent prayer.*

Guide the people of this land, and of all the nations,
in the ways of justice and peace;
that we may honor one another and serve the common good.
Lord, in your mercy, **hear our prayer**. *Silent prayer.*

Give us all a reverence for the earth as your own creation,
that we may use its resources rightly
in the service of others and to your honor and glory.
Lord, in your mercy, **hear our prayer**. *Silent prayer.*

Bless all whose lives are closely linked with ours,
and grant that we may serve Christ in them,
and love one another as Christ loves us.
Lord, in your mercy, **hear our prayer**. *Silent prayer.*

Comfort and heal all those who suffer in body, mind, or spirit;
give them courage and hope in their troubles,
and bring them the joy of your salvation.
Lord, in your mercy, **hear our prayer**. *Silent prayer.*

We commend to your mercy all who have died,
that your will for them may be fulfilled;

and we pray that we may share with all your saints
in your eternal kingdom.
Lord, in your mercy, **hear our prayer**. *Silent prayer.*

We offer these prayers through Jesus Christ our Lord.
Amen.

The Book of Common Prayer, alt.

G.
Living God, Holy Trinity,
whose sovereignty we need and resist,
and fear yet long for:
hear our prayer.
We pray for all who meet and work in this place:
align our purposes with yours,
and lead us by your sovereign love.
We pray for the church, local and worldwide.
Thank you for its dissonant diversity.
Forgive its righteous wrongdoing, inhumanity,
and abuse of power.
Stir up your people's noblest visions;
bring us closer to Christ and each other.
We pray for people of faiths other than our own.
Stir up their noblest visions.
Forgive their sin, and show us their gifts
of wisdom, truth, and peace.
We pray for people in need:
Tame the violence of war and the rhetoric of warmakers;
strengthen peacemakers; comfort those who mourn;
bring food to the hungry, and hope to the oppressed,
and make us hungry and thirsty
for justice, mercy, and kindness.
We pray for institutions, systems, and powers,
local, national, and global,
servants of Christ, yet sinful and corrupt.

...

Restrain their folly, and expose their pretense.
Waken the conscience of the powerful
and the hopes of the weak.
Show us our own captivities
and Christ's resurrection power.
We pray for all living things on earth:
Thank you for all earth's creatures.
Repair the fabric of life.
Restore and renew our creation.
Living and Loving God,
bring all things to completion in Christ,
and bring us home to you,
our source, our goal, our hope, our joy.
In the name of Christ we pray. Amen.

Brian Wren

Variations on the Lord's Prayer

The Lord's Prayer, Traditional

Our Father, who art in heaven,
hallowed be thy name.
Thy kingdom come,
thy will be done on earth as it is in heaven.
Give us this day our daily bread.
And forgive us our trespasses,
as we forgive those who trespass against us.
And lead us not into temptation,
but deliver us from evil.
For thine is the kingdom, and the power, and the glory
forever. Amen.

The United Methodist Hymnal

Ecumenical Version

Our Father in heaven,
hallowed be your name,
your kingdom come,
your will be done,
on earth as in heaven.
Give us today our daily bread.
Forgive us our sins
as we forgive those who sin against us.
Save us from the time of trial
and deliver us from evil.
For the kingdom, the power, and the glory are yours
now and for ever. Amen.

English Language Liturgical Commission

The New Zealand Anglican Lord's Prayer

Eternal Spirit, Earth-maker, Pain-bearer, Life-giver,
Source of all that is and that shall be,
Father and Mother of us all,
Loving God, in whom is heaven:

The hallowing of your name echo through the universe!
The way of your justice be followed by the peoples of the world!
Your heavenly will be done by all created beings!
Your commonwealth of peace and freedom sustain our hope
and come on earth.

With the bread we need for today, feed us.
In the hurts we absorb from one another, forgive us.
In times of temptation and test, strengthen us.
From trials too great to endure, spare us.
From the grip of all that is evil, free us.

For you reign in the glory of the power that is love,
now and for ever. Amen.

A New Zealand Prayer Book – He Karakia Mihinare o Aotearoa

The Lord's Prayer (Matthew 6:9-13, First Nations Version)

O Great Spirit, our Father from above,
we honor your name as sacred and holy.

Bring your good road to us,
where the beauty of your ways in the spirit-world above
is reflected in the earth below.

Provide for us day by day—
the elk, the buffalo, and the salmon.
The corn, the squash, and the wild rice.
All the things we need for each day.

Release us from the things we have done wrong,
in the same way we release others
for the things done wrong to us.

Guide us away from the things
that tempt us to stray from your good road,
and set us free from the evil one and his worthless ways.

Aho! May it be so!

An Indigenous Translation of the New Testament

Prayers of Lament

A. Litany for Welcoming Our Lament

The psalmist declares that an acceptable sacrifice to God is a broken spirit; a broken and contrite heart. Friends, let us bring the fullness of who we are as we enter into a posture of lament today, responding with the word *welcome* after each phrase.

To our grief, we say:
Welcome.
To our anger, we say:
Welcome.
To our despair, we say:
Welcome.
To our sadness, we say:
Welcome.
To our exhaustion, we say:
Welcome.
We welcome our lament together as members of the Family of Christ knowing that we are not alone. To our Companioning God, we say:
Welcome.
Amen.

Another song, prayer, or act of lament may follow.

Lisa Hancock

B. Hear Our Cry

Hear our cry, O God; attend to our prayer. From the depth of our sorrows, we call to you when our hearts are overwhelmed with fears and worries. Lead us to the wings that embrace us in love and peace.

Liturgies from Below

C.

Listening God, with each new day comes fresh news of terror. We lament each new way we find to be inhumane to each other. We lament the numbness many of us feel as we are increasingly desensitized to horror. We sorrow as those harmed by the sin of exclusion and hatred but also as those who are complicit in its execution. We lament the structural sin that can sometimes leave us feeling helpless. But Lord, we aren't helpless. We tear our clothing; we cry aloud, our tears flow, and our hearts break. Hear the deep pain in our hearts. Help us to hear the deep pain in others. But we will ever trust in you, God, our helper and our defender. We will raise our voices, shout out, and not hold back. You call us to justice. Give us courage to pursue it until the day when all the tears will be wiped from our eyes and we look forward in hope. In the name of the One who has heard our cries and delivers us even from ourselves. Amen.

Resist Harm

Offering Prayers

A.

O God, accept our offering of ourselves,
of our time and talents.
Unsettle our lives and redefine them in you.
Renew in us a spirit of justice, compassion and love.
Open our eyes, ears, and hearts
to hear and see you already at work in the world.
Strengthen our commitment to your vision,
through Jesus Christ our Lord. Amen.

Banquet of Praise

B.

Blessed God, you have called us to contribute
to the needs of the saints
and to extend hospitality to strangers.
Hallow these gifts that they may be a blessing
to many in your name. Amen.

Herb Mather

C.

Loving God, faithful and gracious forever,
You love us more than we love ourselves.
You believe in us more than we believe in ourselves.
You call us to walk with Christ,
and be more than we ever thought possible.
Take our gifts.
Receive our thanks.
Accept our praise;
through Jesus Christ. Amen.

Brian Wren

D.

O God, we recognize that we have been blessed
with great abundance.
In offering these gifts, may we be strengthened
to proclaim your faithfulness
and your salvation this day and always.
We pray in the name of Jesus Christ, our Savior. Amen.

David Bell

E.

Lord, we offer you our hearts, our souls, our lives;
everything, for they are already yours. Amen.

Cynthia A. Bond Hopson

Invitations to Christian Discipleship

A. Call to Discipleship (Based on 1 Peter 1:3-9)

We have an opportunity. Let's not miss it. We are called into a living hope through the resurrection of Jesus the Christ. We are called into an imperishable, undefiled, unfading inheritance. Even as you face trials, you are enabled to do so because of Christ's glorious and indescribable joy. Friends, renew your commitment to receive the outcome of faith, that is the salvation of your soul.

Valerie Bridgeman Davis

B. An Invitation to Christ

Come, my Light, and illumine my darkness.
Come, my Life, and revive me from death.
Come, my Physician, and heal my wounds.
Come, Flame of divine love, and burn up the thorns of my sins,
kindling my heart with the flame of thy love.
Come, my King, sit upon the throne
of my heart and reign there.
For thou alone art my King and my Lord. Amen.

Dimitri of Rostov, Russia

Dismissals, Blessings, and Closing Prayers

A.

The grace of the Lord Jesus Christ, the love of God, and the fellowship of the Holy Spirit be with you all.

2 Corinthians 13:13

B.

May the word of Christ dwell in us richly.
Whatever we do in word or deed,
let us do everything in the name of the Lord Jesus,
giving thanks to God. Amen.

Colossians 3:16a, alt.

C.

May the God of peace, who brought back from the dead our Lord Jesus, the great shepherd of the sheep, by the blood of the eternal covenant, make us complete in everything good so that you may do his will, as he works among us that which is pleasing in his sight, through Jesus Christ, to whom be the glory forever. Amen.

Hebrews 13:20-21 NRSVUE

D.

May God bless us and keep us. May God's face shine upon us and be gracious to us. May God lift up the divine countenance upon us, and give us peace. Amen.

Numbers 6:24-26, alt.

E.

The God of all grace, who has called us to eternal glory in Christ, establish and strengthen you by the power of the Holy Spirit, that you may live in grace and peace. Amen.

1 Peter 5:10, alt.

F.

Rejoice in the Lord always; again I say, rejoice.
May the peace of God, which goes
beyond all our understanding,
guard our hearts and our minds in Christ Jesus. Amen.

Philippians 4:4-7, alt.

G.

Friends in Christ,
Bear witness to the love of God in this world,
so that those to whom love is a stranger
will find in you generous friends.
In the name of the Father, Son, and Holy Spirit,
go forth in peace. Amen.

The United Methodist Book of Worship, adapted

H.

God of every beginning,
walk with us in our halting steps.
Prod us forward when we would stop.
Hold us up when we fall.
Love us when we pout because we do not want to change.
Change us into the image of Christ.
Grow us up and out.
May we spread into your grace,
blossom into your joy,
run into your mercy,
this day and always.
Amen.

Valerie Bridgeman Davis

I.

Praise be to the God and Father of our Lord Jesus Christ,
the Father of compassion and the God of all comfort, who
comforts us in all our troubles, so that we can comfort those
in any trouble with the comfort we ourselves have received
from God. (2 Corinthians 1:3-4)

Junius Dotson

J.

Go forth with the authority Christ gives to his church.
Cry out against wrong.
Heal where there is hurt.
Feed, clothe, and defend those who live on the margins.
Train up children in the ways of God.
Show no contempt for youth; comfort the elderly.
In all things, give God the glory and praise, now and forever.
Amen.

Eugene Blair

K.

O God may we receive your blessing,
through sharing your blessings beyond borders.
May we receive your gifts, from those who carry nothing.
May we recognize you, in people we don't know
and may we all find a safe home and peace in you
who had no place to lay your head.

Liturgies from Below

L.

May God keep you safe.
May your bellies be full.
May your thirst be quenched.
May your hearts be blessed with knowing you are loved.
And may you share that love with all who come your way.
Amen.

Liturgies from Below

M.

What does the Lord require of you as you go from this place,
but to do justice, to love mercy, and to walk humbly with God?
In the name of Jesus Christ, go to serve God and your neighbor in all that you do.
Thanks be to God!

Worship in Daily Life

N.

As you have been fed at this table, go to feed the hungry.
As you have been set free, go to set free the imprisoned.
As you have received, give.
As you have heard, proclaim.
And the blessing that you have received
from Father, Son, and Holy Spirit
be always with you. Amen.

Kate McIlhagga

O.

May the love of the Father enfold us,
the wisdom of the Son enlighten us,
and the fire of the Spirit kindle us;
and may the blessing of the Lord God
come down upon us and remain with us always.
Amen.

The Westminster Hymnal

P.

The way is long, let us go together.
The way is difficult, let us help each other.
The way is joyful, let us share it.
The way is Christ's, for Christ is the Way; let us follow.
The way is open before us, let us go:
with the love of God, the grace of Christ,
and the communion of the Holy Spirit. Amen.

James T. Fatzinger

Q.

Living God, in whom we live and move and have our being,
guide and govern us by your Holy Spirit,
so that in all the cares and occupations of our life
we may not forget you,
but remember that we are ever walking in your sight;
through Jesus Christ our Lord. Amen.

The Book of Common Prayer, alt.

R.

Holy Wisdom, in your loving kindness you created us,
restoring us when we were lost.
Inspire us with your truth,
that we may love you with our whole minds
and run to you with open hearts,
through Christ our Savior. Amen.

Alcuin of York

S.

Lord, grant us your blessing.
Kindle in our hearts, O God,
the flame of that love which never ceases,
that it may burn in us, giving light to others.
May we shine forever in your temple,
set on fire with your eternal light,
even your Son Jesus Christ,
our Savior and our Redeemer. Amen.

St. Columba

T.

Before us it is blessed, behind us it is blessed,
below us it is blessed, above us it is blessed,
around us it is blessed as we set out with Christ.
Our speech is blessed as we set out for God.
With beauty before us, with beauty behind us,
with beauty below us, with beauty above us,
with beauty around us, we set out for a holy place indeed.
Amen.

Traditional Navajo Prayer, alt.

Leader (point to ears): May my ears hear you.
Children (repeat): May my ears hear you.
Leader (point to eyes): May my eyes look for you.
Children: May my eyes look for you.
Leader (put hand on chest): May my heart know you.
Children: May my heart know you.
ALL: Amen.

Unknown

Other Acts of Worship on the Lord's Day

Prayer for Church Receiving New Clergy Leader(s)

God of us all, you have sent us [*name(s) of individual(s)*] to work among us as we continue in your love. May [*name(s)*] usher us into another season of following you. You are the Good Shepherd and [*name(s) of individual(s)*] was/were sent to us by the bishop guided by your hand. So, we give you thanks for sending us another one to love us, to pray with and for us, and for this precious individual whom we embrace along with *his/her/their* family. Anoint them and us with the grace needed to continue this journey. Strengthen them for your Holy Work and consecrate them for your glory. Allow your peace and vision to illumine our hearts and minds, so that we may continue to wholly love and serve you and love your people rightly. In Christ's name, we pray. Amen.

Stacey Cole Wilson

A Covenant Prayer in the Wesleyan Tradition

I am no longer my own, but thine.
Put me to what thou wilt, rank me with whom thou wilt.
Put me to doing, put me to suffering.
Let me be employed by thee or laid aside for thee,
exalted for thee or brought low for thee.
Let me be full, let me be empty.
Let me have all things, let me have nothing.

I freely and heartily yield all things
to thy pleasure and disposal.
And now, O glorious and blessed God,
Father, Son, and Holy Spirit,
thou art mine, and I am thine. So be it.
And the covenant which I have made on earth,
let it be ratified in heaven. Amen.

The United Methodist Hymnal

Part Three

Worship Any Time or Place

RESOURCES FOR PASTORS

A Service of Committal

This order is intended primarily for burial in the ground. However, it can be adapted for cremation or the interment of ashes, for burial above ground or at sea, or for donation of the body for medical purposes.

If the family requests that there be military, fraternal, or other rites in addition to the Service of Committal, the pastor should approve such rites and plan carefully the sequence and interrelationship of these services so that the service is not interrupted.

The Lord be with you
And also with you

Blessed be the God and Father of our Lord Jesus Christ, the source of all mercy and the God of all consolation, who comforts us in all our sorrows so that we can comfort others in their sorrows with the consolation we ourselves have received from God. (2 Corinthians 1:3-4)

Friends, we gather now (or "we continue our service of worship") to commend and entrust N. to God's loving embrace. Receive these words of hope from 1 Corinthians 15:

Behold, I will tell you a mystery!
We will not all die, but we will all be changed.
For this perishable body must put on imperishability,
and this mortal body must put on immortality.
Then the saying that is written will be fulfilled:
"Death has been swallowed up in victory."
"Where, O death, is your victory?
Where, O death, is your sting?"
But thanks be to God,
who gives us the victory through our Lord Jesus Christ.

Let us pray.
Holy God, holy and powerful, by the death and burial of
Jesus your anointed, you have destroyed the power of death
and made holy the resting places of all your people. Keep
N., whose body we now lay to rest, in the company of all
your saints. And at the last, O God, raise *her/him/them* up
to share with all the faithful the endless joy and peace won
through the glorious resurrection of Christ our Lord, who
lives and reigns with you and the Holy Spirit, one God, now
and forever. **Amen.**

Receive these words adapted from 1 Peter 1:3-9:

"Blessed be the God and Father of our Lord Jesus Christ!
By his great mercy we have been born anew to a living hope
through the resurrection of Jesus Christ from the dead, and
to an inheritance which is imperishable, undefiled and unfading, kept in heaven for you.
In this you rejoice, though now for a little while you suffer
trials so that the genuineness of your faith may prove itself
worthy at the revelation of Jesus Christ.
Without having seen him, yet you love him;
though you do not now see him,
you believe in him and rejoice
with unutterable and exalted joy.

As the harvest of your faith you reap
the salvation of your souls."

The Word of God for the people of God.
Thanks be to God.

Standing at the head of the coffin and facing it (preferably casting earth upon it as it is lowered into the grave) the pastor says:

Almighty God,
into your hands we commend your *son/daughter/child Name*,
in sure and certain hope of resurrection to eternal life
through Jesus Christ our Lord. **Amen.**

This body we commit to the ground
(to the elements, to the deep, to its resting place),
earth to earth, ashes to ashes, dust to dust.

At this time, you may invite those gathered to commend the deceased by casting earth upon the coffin/urn, or another symbolic gesture. If the gathering is intimate in number, you may encourage those gathered to offer words of blessing and closure to accompany their symbolic gesture. Once all have had the opportunity to participate, the pastor says:

Let us pray.
Eternal God, you have shared with us the life of *Name*.
Before *Name* was ours, *Name* has always belonged to you.
For all that *Name* has given us to make us what we are,
for that of *him/her/them*, which lives and grows in each of us,
and for *his/her/their* life that in your love will never end,
we give you thanks.
As now we offer *Name* back into your arms,
comfort us in our loneliness,
strengthen us in our weakness,
and give us courage to face the future unafraid.

Draw those of us who remain in this life closer to one another,
make us faithful to serve one another,
and help us to know the peace and joy that is eternal life;
through Jesus Christ our Lord. **Amen**.

The Lord's Prayer may follow.

A hymn or song may be sung.

The pastor dismisses the people with the following or another blessing:

Now to the One who is able to keep you from falling,
and to make you stand without blemish
in the presence of God's glory with rejoicing,
to the only God our Savior, through Jesus Christ our Lord,
be glory, majesty, power, and authority,
before all time and now and forever. **Amen**.

If the coffin or urn has not been lowered earlier in the service, it will likely take place at this point. During this time, it is best to offer your support through the ministry of presence.

Renewing Worship
The United Methodist Book of Worship, adapted

A Service of Word and Table V with Persons Who Are Sick or Homebound

Since the earliest Christian times, communion has been brought as an extension of the congregation's worship to sick or homebound persons unable to attend congregational worship.

The following service is very flexible, depending upon the circumstances of the pastoral visit. "The people" may be simply the pastor and one other person. The service may be very informal and conversational. There should be every possible sensitivity to the particular needs of the person(s) receiving communion.

The pastor, or laypersons at the direction of the pastor, may distribute the consecrated bread and cup to sick or homebound persons as soon as feasible following a service of Word and Table as an extension of that service. When this service is used as a distribution of the consecrated bread and cup, the Great Thanksgiving is omitted, but thanks should be given after the bread and cup are received.

There should be whatever participation is feasible by those receiving communion. Sometimes this may simply be gestures and expression. Familiar acts of worship persons may know by memory—the Lord's Prayer, the Apostles' Creed, or the Twenty-third Psalm, for instance—may be used. Sometimes it is possible to sing one or more hymns.

Those distributing communion should also be sensitive to the power of acts such as calling the person by name, touching the person, encouraging the remembrance of significant experiences, and allowing sick or homebound persons to minister to the visitors.

ENTRANCE

The people come together and exchange greetings in the Lord's name.

THE WORD OF GOD

Scriptures are read and interpreted, and prayer and praise are offered.

INVITATION

Christ our Lord invites to his table
all who love him and seek to grow into his likeness.
Let us draw near with faith, make our humble confession,
and prepare to receive this Holy Sacrament.

CONFESSION AND PARDON

**We do not presume to come to this your table,
merciful Lord,
trusting in our own goodness,
but in your unfailing mercies.
We are not worthy that you should receive us,
but give your word and we shall be healed,
through Jesus Christ our Lord. Amen.**

Hear the good news:
Christ died for us while we were yet sinners;
that is proof of God's love toward us.
In the name of Jesus Christ, you are forgiven!

THE PEACE

Signs and words of God's peace are exchanged.

TAKING THE BREAD AND CUP

The bread and wine are prepared for the meal.

THE GREAT THANKSGIVING

*The **pastor** prays as follows **if** the bread and cup are to be consecrated. If they have already been consecrated, this prayer is omitted.
If a layperson is distributing the consecrated bread and cup, this prayer is omitted.*

Lift up your heart(s) and give thanks to the Lord our God.

Father Almighty, Creator of heaven and earth,
you made us in your image, to love and to be loved.
When we turned away, and our love failed,
your love remained steadfast.
By the suffering, death, and resurrection
of your only Son Jesus Christ
you delivered us from slavery to sin and death
and made with us a new covenant by water and the Spirit.

On the night in which Jesus gave himself up for us
he took bread,
gave thanks to you, broke the bread,
gave it to his disciples, and said:
"Take, eat; this is my body which is given for you.
Do this in remembrance of me."

When the supper was over he took the cup,
gave thanks to you, gave it to his disciples, and said:
"Drink from this, all of you;
this is my blood of the new covenant,
poured out for you and for many for the forgiveness of sins.
Do this, as often as you drink it, in remembrance of me."

And so, in remembrance of these
your mighty acts in Jesus Christ,
we offer ourselves in praise and thanksgiving
as a holy and living sacrifice,
in union with Christ's offering for us.
Pour out your Holy Spirit on us,
and on these gifts of bread and wine.
Make them be for us the body and blood of Christ,
that we may be for the world the body of Christ,
redeemed by his blood.

By your Spirit make us one with Christ, one with each other,
and one in ministry to all the world,
until Christ comes in final victory,
and we feast at his heavenly banquet.

Through your Son Jesus Christ,
with the Holy Spirit in your holy Church,
all honor and glory is yours, almighty Father,
now and for ever. Amen.

THE LORD'S PRAYER

BREAKING THE BREAD

In silence or with appropriate words.

GIVING THE BREAD AND CUP

With these or other words being exchanged:

Name, the body of Christ, given for you. **Amen.**

Name, the blood of Christ, given for you. **Amen.**

When all have received, the Lord's table is put in order.

Thanks may be given after communion. A hymn, song, or chorus may be sung. If the **consecrated** *bread and cup from a regular service of Holy Communion have been given and there has been no Great Thanksgiving, the following prayer is suggested after Communion:*

Most bountiful God, we give you thanks
for the world you have created,
for the gift of life, and for giving yourself to us
in Jesus Christ,
whose holy life, suffering and death, and glorious resurrection
have delivered us from slavery to sin and death.
We thank you that in the power of your Holy Spirit
you have fed us in this Sacrament, united us with Christ,
and given us a foretaste of your heavenly banquet.
We are your children, and yours is the glory,
now and for ever;
through Jesus Christ our Lord. **Amen.**

BLESSING

The grace of the Lord Jesus Christ,
and the love of God,
and the communion of the Holy Spirit
be with you [all]. **Amen.**

The United Methodist Book of Worship

A Great Thanksgiving
in Times of Crisis

This prayer utilizes the congregational response: "Come, Lord Jesus!" The presider may offer a physical gesture, such raised hands, or a verbal cue, such as "let us respond" to encourage congregational participation.

God, who holds us all in the palm of your hand:
The circumstances of life are wrenching us away from you.
Call us back! Remind us that you walk with us
and that with you all things are possible.
Come, Lord Jesus!

We remember your Son Jesus standing trial,
being rejected and killed.
In Christ you felt our pain, O God.
Come, Lord Jesus!

Knowing he faced possible death,
Jesus left his followers this reminder
of himself and of your love,
as he said "This is my body given for you.
This is my blood shed for you."
Come, Lord Jesus!

Send your Spirit on these elements
that they may be for us Christ's presence,
broken but whole,
in pain yet in hope.
Come, Lord Jesus! Amen.

Robin Knowles Wallace

Commissioning and Blessing of Newly Licensed Foster Parents

This may also be adapted for a single-parent foster family.

Pastor:
Invite the family members forward and introduce them.
We rejoice that the _____ family has been approved and licensed as a foster home. Let us bless them and pray for them as they begin this important ministry.

In God's Word, we read: "True devotion, the kind that is pure and faultless before God the Father, is this: to care for orphans and widows in their difficulties and to keep the world from contaminating us" (James 1:27).

In another place we read: "Sing to God! Sing praises to his name! . . . Father of orphans and defender of widows is God in his holy habitation. God settles the lonely in their homes" (Psalm 68:4-6).

Pastor to Foster Family:

_____ (*names*), you have heard the call of God to care for the most vulnerable among us—children who, through no fault of their own, find themselves separated from families who have failed them. Will you rely on the power and grace of God to provide these precious children a haven of encouragement, safety, and healing? To help them learn to trust again? To live a life that reminds them they are loved and valued, not simply by you, but by others and by their Father in heaven?

Foster Family:
We will.

Pastor to Congregation:
Will you support this family in their calling? Will you commit to praying for their family and welcoming their children to this community?

Congregation:
We will

At this time, the foster parents/family may kneel or stand in the aisle among the congregation. The congregation is invited to rise, move, and lay hands of blessing and support on the foster parents/family. Anointing with oil is optional.

Pastor:
Let us pray:
God of Grace, we praise you and thank you that you do not leave us orphaned, but welcome all into your family. Shower your blessings upon _____ (*names*) as they prepare to receive foster children into their homes and hearts. Prepare and equip them to love these children with Christlike love. Give them patience to deal with the challenges that are to come. Grant them wisdom to guide and direct the young lives in their charge. When the time comes for the children to move on, fill all involved with peace and hope and trust in the future, knowing they remain forever in your steadfast care.

We ask all this in the strong name of Jesus, the One who brings new life, the One who taught us to pray . . . (*conclude with the Lord's Prayer*).

or

We ask all this in the strong name of Jesus, the One who brings new life. Amen.
John Gill, adapted by Lisa Ann Moss Degrenia and Nelson Cowan

A Covenant Affirmation after an Autism Diagnosis

As a response to the word and/or during a remembrance of baptism service, invite the autistic person* (and their family, if appropriate) to collaborate on ways to express their creativity, gifts, and individuality throughout the ritual. This requires a highly individualized approach**, but would allow the congregation and the autistic person and their family an opportunity to integrate their whole identity—autism and all—into the life of the church. It could be best to invite just the individual's most trusted family members or friends to participate together.

Creator God, divergent Jesus, gifting Spirit:
You who knit us all together
in our mother (or parent)'s womb;
You who wove beautiful diversity
into every part of your creation,
including our human minds, and called it good;
You who remind us that the body of Christ is whole
only as long as it is accessible for us all to be included;
Give *N.* the confidence to be themself in this space.
Draw near to *N.* and their family as they discover what it
means to live into their autistic identity,
as they grieve any losses of a future hoped for,
and celebrate the hope of the future they now see more clearly.
Teach us how to love one another better as we embrace *N.*,
to joyfully make room for their gifts,
and promise to patiently endure
beside them the challenges
of this newly revealed part of their identity.
Amen.

This ritual uses "identity-first" language. If someone prefers "person-first" language, the language here should be adapted to respect that preference.

**If appropriate, ask the individual their favorite celebratory gesture and include instructions in the bulletin on how to join the individual in celebrating after "amen." Another possibility would be to adapt the prayer to allow the autistic individual to lead the congregation using their preferred method of communication.

Perrin Crouch

An Order for the Installation of Church Leaders

This order may be included in a service of worship when elected or appointed leaders among the laity in the congregation are to be installed or recognized.

As a Response to the Word or at some other appropriate place within a public worship service, the pastor invites the leaders being recognized to come forward. The pastor presents the leaders to the congregation and then says to them:

Dear friends,
you have been called by God
and chosen by the people of God
for leadership in the church.
This ministry is a blessing and a serious responsibility.
It recognizes your special gifts
and calls you to work among us and for us.
In love we thank you for accepting your obligation
and challenge you to offer your best
to the Lord, to this people, and to our ministry in the world.
Live a life in Christ
and make him known in your witness and your work.

Today we install (recognize) *Names*.
Do you this day acknowledge yourself a faithful disciple of
Jesus Christ?

I do.

Will you devote yourself to the service of God in the world?

I will.

Will you so live
that you enable this church to be a people of love and
peace?

I will.

Will you do all in your power
to be responsible to the task for which you have been
chosen?

I will.

Let us pray.
Almighty God, pour out your blessings upon these your
servants
who have been given particular ministries in your church.

Grant them grace to give themselves wholeheartedly in
your service.

Keep before them the example of our Lord,
who did not think first of himself, but gave himself for us all.

Let them share his ministry and consecration,
that they may enter into his joy.

Guide them in their work.

Reward their faithfulness with the knowledge
that through them your purposes are accomplished;
through Jesus Christ our Lord. Amen.

The pastor addresses the congregation:

Dear friends,
rejoice that God provides laborers for the vineyards.
Will you do all you can to assist and encourage them
in the responsibilities to which they have been called,
giving them your cooperation, your counsel,
and your prayers?

The congregation responds:
We will.

The pastor may greet the leaders individually.

The United Methodist Book of Worship

Prayer for Godspeed: A Service of Farewell for Departing Members

On the Sunday prior to their moving, the pastor may announce at an appropriate time in the service, perhaps near the conclusion of the service, that N (family/individual/group) will soon be moving. The family/individual/group may be invited to come forward to present themselves to the congregation.

INTRODUCTION

The pastor addresses the congregation:

The Scriptures are filled with stories of people
who have been called to move to new places:
Abraham and Sarah, Mary and Joseph,
Paul and Barnabas, Priscilla and Aquila.
Filled with uncertainty about what lay ahead,
these people of God could not have found their moves easy.
Yet they were also filled with excitement,
trusting that God was calling them
and guiding them to a new place.

And now you, our beloved friend/s,
are preparing to leave us
and go to a new place, a new home, and a new church.
As a part of this body of Christ over the past years,
you have given of *yourselves/yourself*
in ways that we have appreciated and will miss.

[*If leaving because of disaffiliation, you may add:* We lament that we could not remain one body, but we honor your wishes to depart.]

AFFIRMATIONS

Here the pastor may mention the gifts and qualities of those who are moving as well as their specific contributions to the life of the church.

FAREWELL BLESSING

We ask God's blessing upon you as we lift our hearts in prayer. *The pastor may invite the rest of the congregation to offer a physical gesture of blessing, such as outstretched arms.*

Let us pray.
Blessed are you, O God,
for you have created the wide and wonderful world
in which we live.
We praise you for your constant care
for those who have trusted you in ages past,
who journeyed in faith to new lands of promise.
We trust that now you will hold *N*_____
(or "this group of people")
securely in your hands as *they,* too,
follow/s your call to a new place.
May *they* take with *them*
hearts filled with your love and grace,
that those with whom *they* live and work
may see in *them* the face of Jesus Christ.

Bless them that *they* may be a blessing.
Guide *them* to a new church home,
where *they* may continue to grow
in grace, in Spirit, and in truth;
through Jesus Christ our Lord.
Amen.

DISMISSAL WITH BLESSING

Now, may the God of peace,
who brought back the great shepherd of the sheep,
our Lord Jesus,
from the dead by the blood of the eternal covenant,
equip you with every good thing to do his will,
by developing in us what pleases him through Jesus Christ.
To him be the glory forever and always. Amen.

> *Prayer for Godspeed: A Service of Farewell,*
> *The Reformed Church in America, adapted.*

A Service for the Blessing of Animals

A Blessing of Animals, in many congregations, witnesses to God's and the Church's love, care, and concern for creation. As we recognize our mutual interdependence with God's creatures, the Church's witness of stewardship of creation is strengthened. It is also a service with special appeal to children.

The Blessing is best celebrated during daylight in the outdoors—in the churchyard or in a park. It may be celebrated at any time of the year, especially in early spring, or on the Feast Day of St. Francis of Assisi, October 4. Make allowances for the arrival of larger animals such as horses and other livestock. The space may contain a table on which the Bible or musical instruments may be placed. Music is best led by instruments that work well outdoors. Bulletins can be awkward and should be used only to provide the texts of hymns to be sung.

GATHERING AND GREETING

The Lord be with you
And also with you.
Let us pray.

Holy Creator, give us eyes to see and ears to hear how every living thing speaks to us of your love. Enable us to rejoice that we are alive among so many miracles and give us a spirit of gratitude and responsibility for all your creatures, for we pray in the name of Jesus who lay in a cow's manger when he was born, who told a parable about the kindness of dogs, and who came to Jerusalem on a borrowed donkey. Amen.

HYMN SUGGESTIONS

"All Creatures of Our God and King"
"All Things Bright and Beautiful"
"This Is My Father's World"
"Morning Has Broken"

SCRIPTURE

Receive the Word of the Lord from Genesis, chapter 1, verses 24 and 25 NRSVUE:
God said: "Let the earth bring forth living creatures of every kind: cattle and creeping things and wild animals of the earth of every kind." And it was so. God made the wild animals of the earth of every kind and the cattle of every kind and everything that creeps upon the ground of every kind. And God saw that it was good.
Amen.

In Psalm 50, God declares: "I will take no bull-calf from your stalls; nor he-goats out of your pens; for all the beasts of the forest are mine; the herds in their thousands upon the hills. I know every bird in the sky; and the creatures of the fields are in my sight."

The Word of God for the people of God.
Thanks be to God.

WORDS OF REFLECTION

Depending on the context, it may be suitable to use or adapt the words below, offer a brief homily, or skip ahead to prayer of blessing.

The animals of God's creation
inhabit the skies, the earth, and the sea.
They share in the fortunes of human existence
and have a part in human life.
God, who confers gifts on all living things,
has often used the service of animals
or made them reminders of the gifts of salvation.
Animals were saved from the flood
and afterward made a part of the covenant with Noah.
The paschal lamb recalls the Passover sacrifice
and the deliverance from slavery in Egypt.
A giant fish saved Jonah,
ravens brought bread to Elijah,
animals were included in the repentance of Nineveh,
and animals share in Christ's redemption
of all God's creation.
We, therefore, invoke God's blessing on these animals.

PRAYER OF BLESSING

Instrumental music or the singing of hymns may accompany this time of blessing. It is preferable for the minister/worship leader to visit each animal, rather than making animals come forward. The minister / worship leader then asks the name of the animal, places their hand on the animal's head (if appropriate), and then blesses the animal:

[*Animal Name*], you were created by God, and you are loved by God. May you and your human family experience joy and companionship together, and continue to be a blessing to each other. In the name of the Father, Son, and Holy Spirit. Amen.

DISMISSAL WITH BLESSING

May God, who created the animals of this earth,
continue to protect and sustain us all,
now and forever. **Amen.**

> *The United Methodist Book of Worship, adapted with resources from Maren C. Tirabassi, Barbara Allen, and Nelson Cowan*

A Service for the Blessing of a Home

GATHERING

Family and friends gather inside or outside the home.

GREETING

The leader addresses the family and friends:

Dear friends,
we have gathered here to seek God's blessing upon this home.

This home is not only a dwelling,
but a symbol to us of God's loving provision
and of our life together as the family of Christ.
We gather joyfully in the name of Jesus, who said:
"Listen! I am standing at the door, knocking;
if you hear my voice and open the door, I will come in."

OPENING PRAYER

Let us pray.
Almighty and everlasting God,
grant to this home the grace of your presence,
that you may be known to inhabit this dwelling
and defend this household;
through Jesus Christ our Lord,
who with you and the Holy Spirit
lives and reigns, one God, for ever and ever. **Amen.**

SCRIPTURE

Matthew 7:24-27

"Everybody who hears these words of mine and puts them into practice is like a wise builder who built a house on bedrock. The rain fell, the floods came, and the wind blew and beat against that house. It didn't fall because it was firmly set on bedrock. But everybody who hears these words of mine and doesn't put them into practice will be like a fool who built a house on sand. The rain fell, the floods came, and the wind blew and beat against that house. It fell and was completely destroyed."

The Word of the Lord.
Thanks be to God.

CONSECRATION OF THE HOME

In the name of the Father, and of the Son,
and of the Holy Spirit
(in the name of the holy and triune God),
we consecrate this home,
committing to God's love and care all
(the one) who dwell(s) therein.
Amen.

Let us pray.
Eternal God, bless this home.
Let your love rest upon it
and your promised presence be manifested in it.
May the members of this household (*Name*)
grow in grace and in the knowledge of our Lord Jesus Christ.
Teach them (him, her) to love, as you have loved us;
and help us all to live in the peace of Jesus Christ our Lord.
Amen.

The service may conclude with the Lord's Prayer and Dismissal with Blessing.

The United Methodist Book of Worship, adapted

RESOURCES FOR ALL MINISTERS

Rhythms of the Calendar Year

Beginning a New Year
(Heb. 11:1-2 and Phil. 3:12-15)

God of new beginnings,
we rejoice in your presence in this new year.
We praise you for the opportunity to serve you together.
Through your Spirit, empower us to press forward
toward the high goal
you have given us in Jesus Christ.
Lift from our shoulders every weight that holds us back,
and free us from all failings that tempt us from the way,
that we may faithfully fulfill the callings you set before us.
We pray through Jesus Christ,
the pioneer and perfecter of our faith,
who has run the race before us
and continues beside us forever. Amen.

Ruth Duck

For Martin Luther King Jr. Day

Most gracious and all wise God, before whose face the generations rise and fall; Thou in whom we live, and move, and
have our being. We thank thee [for] all of thy good and

gracious gifts, for life and for health; for food and for raiment; for the beauties of nature and human nature. We come before thee painfully aware of our inadequacies and shortcomings. We realize that we stand surrounded with the mountains of love and we deliberately dwell in the valley of hate. We stand amid the forces of truth and deliberately lie. We are forever offered the high road and yet we choose to travel the low road. For these sins, O God, forgive. Break the spell of that which blinds our minds. Purify our hearts that we may see thee. O God, in these turbulent days when fear and doubt are mounting high, give us broad visions, penetrating eyes, and power of endurance. Help us to work with renewed vigor for a warless world, for a better distribution of wealth and for a brother/sisterhood that transcends race or color. In the name and spirit of Jesus we pray. Amen.

Martin Luther King Jr.

Earth Day Prayer of Confession

O God, maker of heaven and earth,
of all that is, seen and unseen:
You place us in your creation,
and you command us to care for it.
Your works declare glory and splendor,
and you call us to praise and reverence.
Where we have degraded or destroyed earth's bounty,
forgive us.
Where we have taken beauty and majesty for granted,
have mercy upon us.
Where we have become estranged from the creatures
with whom we share this planet, grant us your peace.

Renew us in the waters of baptism,
refresh us with the winds of your spirit,
and sustain us with the bread of life.
In the name of Jesus Christ,
and for the sake of the new creation, we pray. Amen.

Ken Carter

For Mother's Day

God, both mother and father for humankind and creation,
we are grateful and thankful today for mothering;
for the feminine touch of parenting,
for the special connection of mother and child,
and thankful for all the women in our lives,
who offer care, comfort, encouragement and support.
We are grateful for the self-sacrifice of love that is given,
and we offer our love in return.
We remember the mothers who are.
We remember the mothers who have been and are gone.
We remember the mothers who can't be.
We acknowledge that mothering is hard,
And not all are able to do so as they would like.
We acknowledge that we all fall short in life and love,
And that mothers are no exception in this.
However, today, we honor mothering,
Especially those who give of their best.
We pray for mothers all, and those who offer mothering
beyond the circle of bloodlines and family.
For mothers and motherers we pray.
Amen.

Jon Humphries

For Memorial Day

Our holy and gracious God, help us to remember.
Help us to remember the sacrifices bravely made
in which one has given life for another and for all.
Help us to remember those that stand in the breach
where there is trouble
and in which conflict threatens to undo your good creation.
Help us to remember that we look for the day
when every sword will be replaced by a plow,
that all may be fed and live in your peace.
Forgive us every sin that makes for division and for war,
and bring us all into your kingdom on earth as in heaven.
This we pray in Jesus' name. Amen.

Doug Paysour

For Father's Day

Heavenly Father, you entrusted your Son Jesus, the child of Mary, to the care of Joseph, an earthly father. Bless all fathers as they care for their families. Give them strength and wisdom, tenderness and patience; support them in the work they have to do, protecting those who look to them, as we look to you for love and salvation, through Jesus Christ our rock and defender.

Prayers of The Church of England, Author Unknown

Juneteenth: A Pouring of Libations

The pouring of libations may be offered by pouring fresh water in to a living plant of appropriate size. The offering of water as sign and source of life, poured (offered) giving up some of what

98

has been so graciously given acknowledging: After each pouring the gathered people say "Ashe" (Ahshay) or Amen.

The gathered people may be invited to lift up names of ancestors, those to be remembered at the appropriate times. Every generation (elders, infants, teens, children, young adults, middle age) should be represented as a gathered visible presence as libations are poured.

First Pouring: to acknowledge God our source, our Creator, the giver of Life.

Second Pouring: to acknowledge the full presence of God with us Source, Savior and Holy Spirit.

Third Pouring: to acknowledge our ancestors, the great cloud of witnesses now one with God.

Fourth Pouring: to acknowledge the generations that fought died and led us to freedom from slavery persecution, Jim Crow laws, inequitable access to rights and resources in this society.

Fifth Pouring: to acknowledge, those who have led the struggle for freedom in recent times and even now. We name them with our voices and in our hearts as we pour thanking God.

Sixth Pouring: to acknowledge our children and our children's children. The generations of hope and promise entrusted to us by the Grace of God. We pour in thanksgiving and in Hope.

Seventh Pouring: to acknowledge God our Source, Our Savior Jesus the Christ, Our Sustainer and Counsel and Comforter the Holy Spirit.
Thanks Be to God.

Prayer for Our Country
(Suitable for Independence Day
or Other Patriotic Observances)

While this prayer was written for the United States, it can be suitable for other countries and adapted accordingly.

God bless our country
with humility and wisdom,
to hear your voice
not in triumph over others
but in love for one another,
for all who, for every reason,
find themselves upon this land.
May our patriotism be care for all,
not just for one family or place or kind.
Give us courage to face injustice,
to resist the powers that diminish life,
to repent of hate, and heal oppression,
for the sake of liberty and justice for all.
Bless us with prosperity of gratitude,
freedom of love and abundance of generosity.
For the land and water that so richly provide for us
we give thanks and pray for healing and renewal.
Bless us all that we may truly belong to the land,
to one another, and to you,
in a spirit of unity, gratitude and joy.
Amen.

Steve Garnaas-Holmes

For Independence Day

Almighty God, you rule all the peoples of the earth.
Inspire the minds of all to whom you have committed
the responsibility of government and leadership
in the nations of the world.
Give to them the vision of truth and justice,
that by their counsel
all nations and peoples may work together.
Give to the people of our country
zeal for justice and strength of forbearance,
that we may use our liberty
in accordance with your gracious will.
Forgive our shortcomings as a nation;
purify our hearts to see and love the truth.
We pray all these things through Jesus Christ. Amen.

Andy Langford

Back to School Blessing

Bless my paper and my pen.
Guide my spirit deep within.
Help me think and help me play,
this whole school year, day by day.

As I move from class to class,
guide my footsteps; clear my path.
Keep my tongue to speak your words.
Let your will for me be heard.

In every subject high or low,
may God's excellence be shown!
Keep me strong to reach the prize,
to grow in grace, becoming wise.

Whether far from home or near,
may I hold God's precepts dear.
To do my best at every task;
for this blessing, I do ask.

Help my family be a part
as I lift my mind and heart.
As I study, work, and pray,
be with them throughout the day.

Of whom much is given, much is required.
May learning be your greatest desire!

Marilyn E. Thornton

A Blessing of the Backpacks (Intergenerational)

This can be prayed by one leader, or in a "repeat after me" style with the leader and the children.

Caring God . . .
we offer these backpacks . . .
as a sign of our thanks . . .
for all you will do . . .
with us and for us . . .
this year at school. . . .
We bless these backpacks . . .
as companions to us . . .
as we learn and grow. . . .
May they carry . . .
food for bodies . . .
and food for thought. . . .
Let them be a reminder . . .
that you are as close to us . . .

as the backpack on our back . . .
always . . .
and . . .
forever. . . .
Amen!

Marcia McFee

A Blessing for Workers and All Seeking Work (Suitable for Labor Day)

Blessed are you, ever-creating God,
in your image, our lives are made;
in your glory, we offer all the work
of our hearts and hands and minds.
Blessed are you, O God, now and forever!

Blessed are you whose work is repaid,
for by your work, and by the payment you receive
your lives and the lives of others around you
and around the world are blessed.
We thank God for you day by day.

Blessed are you whose work is unpaid,
who offer what you can to enrich the lives of others,
through time, talents, skill, strength, and love.
We praise God for your generous labor!

Blessed are you who seek work but have not found it,
or whose work now is not yet what it may be
yet still you seek, that your gifts may be shared more fully.
We praise God for your diligent seeking
and pray you may soon find!

Yours is the glory in their labors.
Yours be the glory in all our lives, in Jesus' name. Amen.

United Methodist Communications

For Indigenous Peoples' Day

O Great Spirit, God of every people and every tribe, we come to you as your many children, to ask for your forgiveness and guidance. Forgive us for the colonialism that stains our past, the ignorance that allowed us to think that we could claim another's home for our own.

Heal us of this history.

Remind us that none of us were discovered since none of us were lost, but that we are all gathered within the sacred circle of your community.

Guide us through your wisdom to restore the truth of our heritage. Help us to confront the racism that divides us as we confess the pain it has caused to the human family. . . .

Call us to kinship. Mend the hoop of our hearts and let us live in justice and peace . . . through Jesus Christ . . . the one who comes that all people might live with dignity. . . . Amen.

The Episcopal Church Office of Indigenous Ministries

For Veterans Day

Merciful God, you grieve amid the pain, fear, and suffering of your children. Look with compassion on all who endure the miseries of war. Be mindful, too, of those who day and night face peril in defense of our nation. Guide them in their duties as they seek justice of our nation. Guide them in their duties as they seek justice for those subjected to tyranny and liberty for those who are oppressed. Eternal Protector of the helpless, hear the cry of the distressed and grant speedy deliverance in a new day of peace and concord. Amen.

Prayer Book for the Armed Services

A Thanksgiving Prayer

God, there are days we do not feel grateful. When we are anxious or angry. When we feel alone. When we do not understand what is happening in the world or with our neighbors. When the news is bleak, confusing. God, we struggle to feel grateful.

But this Thanksgiving, we choose gratitude.

We choose to accept life as a gift from you, and as a gift from the unfolding work of all creation.

We choose to be grateful for the earth from which our food comes; for the water that gives life; and for the air we all breathe.

We choose to thank our ancestors, those who came before us, grateful for their stories and struggles, and we receive their wisdom as a continuing gift for today.

We choose to see our families and friends with new eyes, appreciating and accepting them for who they are. We are thankful for our homes, whether humble or grand.

We will be grateful for our neighbors, no matter how they voted, whatever our differences, or how much we feel hurt or misunderstood by them.

We choose to see the whole planet as our shared commons, the stage of the future of humankind and creation.

God, this Thanksgiving, we do not give thanks. We choose it. We make this choice of thanks with courageous hearts, knowing that it is humbling to say "thank you." We choose to see your sacred generosity, aware that we live in an infinite circle of gratitude. That we all are guests at a hospitable table around which gifts are passed and received. We will not let anything opposed to love take over this table. Instead, we choose grace, free and unmerited love, the giftedness of life everywhere. In this choosing, and in the making, we will pass gratitude onto the world.

Thus, with you, and with all those gathered at this table, we pledge to make thanks. We ask you to strengthen us in this resolve. Here, now, and into the future. Around our family table. Around the table of our nation. Around the table of the earth.

We choose thanks.

Amen.

Diana Butler Bass

Recognizing the Longest Night at Home

A Blue Christmas Service is offered especially for those hurting during the holidays. It's often offered on December 21, the longest night of the year. You may not have such a service in your area or be able to get to a service due to weather, health, or some other circumstance. There are many reasons you may need a remembrance like this at this time of year. Maybe you're mourning the death of a loved one. Maybe you're far from home. Maybe you or someone you love is suffering from illness, addiction, or estrangement. Maybe you're lonely, struggling financially, or in conflict with someone. Maybe you're recovering from a storm or other natural disaster. Maybe you're hurting because of the great pain, need, and violence in our nation and world.

This is a moment, a safe space, to acknowledge the truth of what we're feeling and going through. Here we don't have to be strong. This is a moment to pause in the midst of suffering to remember God is good. God is strong. God is near. We are not alone and we have every reason to hold on to hope.

SET-UP

A quiet place by yourself or with others
Soft, instrumental music to play in the background
A candle to light
Optional: tissues, journal/paper, and writing instrument

OPENING PRAYER

Merciful God,
In this season of rejoicing, we come to you weary and grieving
In this season of feasting, we hunger for healing and relief
In this season of light, our hearts are veiled
in sorrow and shadow
Will this season ever end?

"Yes." We hear your yes.
Those who are weary will find rest
Those who mourn will be comforted
Those who hunger will be filled
The Light shines in the darkness,
and the darkness will not overcome it.

LIGHTING THE CHRIST CANDLE
Strike a match and light a candle

We welcome you O Christ, Light of the World. In the midst
of our suffering, help us to worship you in spirit and in truth.

SCRIPTURE: ISAIAH 11:1-5
A shoot will grow up from the stump of Jesse;
a branch will sprout from his roots.
The LORD's spirit will rest upon him,
a spirit of wisdom and understanding,
a spirit of planning and strength,
a spirit of knowledge and fear of the LORD.
He will delight in fearing the LORD.

He won't judge by appearances,
nor decide by hearsay.
He will judge the needy with righteousness,
and decide with equity for those who suffer in the land.
He will strike the violent with the rod of his mouth;
by the breath of his lips he will kill the wicked.
Righteousness will be the belt around his hips,
and faithfulness the belt around his waist.

Pause to reflect on the scripture reading. Journal or doodle if you like.

PRAYER: In the Light of God's Love
This candle represents our suffering
and the suffering of the world.
In the light of God's love, we claim God's gift of truth.
There is no need to hide or deny.
God welcomes us as we are.
"Incline your ear, O LORD, and answer me,
for I am poor and needy" (Psalm 86:1 ESV).

Pause to reflect, journal, or doodle.

This candle represents our suffering
and the suffering of the world.
In the light of God's love, we claim God's gift of lament.
We recognize our wounds and cry out to God.
We accept God's invitation
to express every feeling and question.
"My God, my God, why have you forsaken me? Why are
you so far from helping me, from the words of my groaning?
O my God, I cry by day, but you do not answer; and by
night, but find no rest" (Psalm 22:1-2 NRSVUE).

Offer your lament to God silently, out loud, or in your journal.
Be honest and specific.

This candle represents our suffering
and the suffering of the world.
In the light of God's love, we claim God's gift of courage.
Courage to be honest, to seek help, to comfort one another.
Courage to dare to love and dream again.
"The Lord is my strength and my shield; in him my heart
trusts; so I am helped, and my heart exults, and with my
song I give thanks to him" (Psalm 28:7 NRSVUE).

Continue to pray silently, out loud, or in your journal.

This candle represents our suffering
and the suffering of the world.
In the light of God's love, we claim God's gift of hope.
God is good. God is strong. God is near,
leading us to a day without tears and pain,
without sin and death.
Healing and deliverance are coming;
if not now, then on that day.
"By awesome deeds you answer us with deliverance, O God
of our salvation; you are the hope of all the ends of the earth
and of the farthest seas" (Psalm 65:5 NRSVUE).
Jesus, you are full of compassion, you understand our pain.
Our suffering changes our experience of you and the celebration of your birth. We are caught between remembering
happier times and grieving what might have been. In our
loss, we feel cut off—disconnected, adrift, alone.
Root us in your steadfast love.
Anchor us in your faithful promises.
Hold us, and all who weep this holy season
throughout the world.

Offer prayers for the world

PRAYER: For Grace to Bear Suffering

I pray for the grace to bear my sufferings
as Christ bore his for me—
with dignity, humility, forgiveness.
I pray for the grace to bear my sufferings
as Christ bore his for me—
with compassion, truth, endurance.
I pray for the grace to bear my sufferings
as Christ bore his for me—
knowing my sufferings are not like his, and not like others,
yet shared with the universal longings of all humanity,
real and painful and deep.
No need for comparison; only companionship.
I pray for the grace to bear my sufferings
as Christ bore his for me,
as Christ bore his for all.
All I will ever suffer, all we all will ever suffer
will be made known, will be made whole,
through his love and self-giving.
In this, I believe, and trust, and follow, and hope.
In this, I am made new.
Thanks be to God! Hallelujah! Amen!

Lisa Ann Moss Degrenia

Waking and Sleeping

An Examen in the Wesleyan Tradition

The examen is rooted in Ignatian spirituality. It invites us to reflect on the events of the day in effort to discern God's will and direction for us.

GRACE

I begin today by claiming my identity
as one who is created in the image of God.
I am fearfully and wonderfully made.
I am of sacred worth and am uniquely gifted.
When I come to myself—the truth of who I am—
I experience blessing.
I reflect on those persons
who have been a part of my life today,
who have seen this in me, who have encouraged me.
Have I really been attentive to them?
Have I fully accepted their gifts?
I stay with these encounters for a moment.
I see the faces of these persons and listen to their voices again.

REPENTANCE

Next, I see the moments of my day that I regret.
I rely upon the fruit of the Holy Spirit,
especially love, peace, and patience,
for help in returning to these moments.
This is uncomfortable.
And yet repentance that is of God
is a return to the love God wants for me.
It is the journey home.

For a moment, I consider the ways I am stuck or lost.
Why do I resist change?
I ask for the courage to return to God.

CONFESSION

As I reflect on the day, I ask God to reveal the harm
that I have done to others
and the harm I have done to myself.
I make an honest assessment of my failures and mistakes.
Where I have not loved my neighbor as myself, I confess
that I have sinned.
What is the sin that separates me from those closest to me?
How does arrogance, judgmentalism,
ego or privilege distort the way I see others?
How have I buried my birthright gifts
and refused to enjoy and share them?

FAITH

I ask for the gift of God's healing and renewing grace.
I set aside my own claims of righteousness or merit.
In faith, I say yes to Jesus Christ,
who loves me and gave himself for me.
I place my trust in Jesus Christ alone for the gift of salvation.
And for a moment, I consider
how I am actually living by faith.
Do I find it difficult to trust?
I return to the good news that I embraced
when I first began to walk with Jesus.
I ask that God would empower me to live this day in faith.

LOVE

God has created me. God knows me.
God's sacrificial love in the crucified Jesus is for my salvation.

When I have received the gift of faith,
I become a more loving person.
And when I have placed my faith and trust in Jesus Christ,
I become a part of his body, which is the church.
I boldly ask that I will be made perfect in love in this life—
that I will love God
and love the people I encounter each day in God.
I ask that my love for God would grow as I read the scriptures,
spend time in prayer
and receive communion as often as possible.
I ask God to give me a greater love for others,
especially those to whom
I have made promises and covenants,
and those with whom I have differences.
I ask God for the happiness
is taking the daily risk of living in grace,
practicing repentance and confession,
and growing in a faith that expresses itself through love.
Amen.

Ken Carter

O Gracious Light (Phos Hilaron)

O gracious light,
pure brightness of the everliving Father in heaven,
O Jesus Christ, holy and blessed!

Now as we come to the setting of the sun,
and our eyes behold the vesper light,
we sing your praises, O God: Father, Son, and Holy Spirit.

You are worthy at all times to be praised by happy voices,
O Son of God, O Giver of life,
and to be glorified through all the worlds.

The Book of Common Prayer

A Prayer before Sleeping (A)

O God,
the life of all who live, the light of the faithful,
the strength of those who labor,
and the repose of the dead,
we thank you for the blessings of the day that is past
and humbly ask for your protection through the coming night.
Bring us in safety to the morning hours;
through him who died and rose again for us,
our Savior Jesus Christ. Amen.

Mozarabic Sacramentary

A Prayer before Sleeping (B)

O Lord,
support us all the day long of this troublous life,
until the shadows lengthen and the evening comes,
and the busy world is hushed,
and the fever of life is over, and our work is done.
Then in your mercy grant us a safe lodging,
and a holy rest, and peace at the last. Amen.

John Henry Newman

A Prayer upon Waking (A)

ADONAI, passionate presence, mystery here and holy,
known in relationship and revealed in a thousand stories:
awaken us each morning to your indwelling, and at days end,
hide us under the shadow of your wings. Amen.

Dan Benedict

A Prayer upon Waking (B)

Lord of the morning
I awake to
this new day
with all of its possibilities,
its uncertainties,
its many faces,
and its underlying
mystery.
May I be able—
in your strength—
to move
through this day
free of anger
or bitterness,
so that
when I meet my neighbor
or encounter the stranger,
I may recognize
your face.

Peter W. Millar

A Prayer upon Waking (C)

This prayer was written for those who are ill but can be applicable for all.

This is another day, O Lord. I know not what it will bring forth, but make me ready, Lord, for whatever it may be. If I am to stand up, help me to stand bravely. If I am to sit still, help me to sit quietly. If I am to lie low, help me to do it patiently. And if I am to do nothing, let me do it gallantly. Make these words more than words, and give me the Spirit of Jesus. Amen.

The Book of Common Prayer

Interpersonal Prayers / Blessings

A Blessing for a Wedding Engagement

God of new beginnings,
you have caused your love to grow between *N.* and *N.*
As they begin to imagine their future together,
fill them with delight and joy.
Give them strength and patience for the planning ahead.
Most of all, let them experience the coming days
as holy and treasured time.
In Jesus' name. Amen.

Inclusive Marriage Services: A Wedding Sourcebook

A Blessing for Newlyweds

Eternal God,
without your grace no promise is sure.
Strengthen *N.* and *N.* with patience, kindness, gentleness,
and all other gifts of your Spirit,
so that they may continue to fulfill the vows they have made.
Keep them faithful to each other and to you.
Fill them with such love and joy
that they may build a home of peace and welcome.
Guide them by your Word to serve you all their days.
Help us all, O God,
to do your will in each of our homes and lives.
Enrich us with your grace so that, supporting one another,
we may serve those in need
and hasten the coming of peace,
love, and justice on earth,
through Jesus Christ our Lord. Amen.

Inclusive Marriage Services: A Wedding Sourcebook

An Anniversary Blessing

God of the journey,
through the years, you have walked with *N.* and *N.*
You have provided them with laughter and joy,
and given them strength and courage in times of trouble.
Continue to bless their life together,
that their love might find new depths
and lead them around surprising corners.
May their love unearth their deepest integrity,
that in their union, they might truly find
whom God has created them to be.
Bless them in the years ahead, and on the last day
bring them into the joy of heaven, where love will never end.
In the name of Jesus Christ we pray. Amen.

Inclusive Marriage Services: A Wedding Sourcebook

A Prayer for Someone
Going through a Divorce

God of infinite love and understanding,
pour out your healing Spirit upon *Name,*
as *he/she/they* reflect[s] upon the failure/ending
of *his/her/their* marriage
and make[s] a new beginning.

Where there is hurt or bitterness,
grant healing of memories
and the ability to put behind the things that are past.

Where feelings of despair or worthlessness flood in,
nurture the spirit of hope and confidence
that by your grace tomorrow can be better than yesterday.

Where [*Name*] looks within and discovers faults
that have contributed to the destruction of the marriage
and have hurt other people,
grant forgiveness for what is past
and growth in all that makes for new life.

[Heal *children's names*,
and help us minister your healing to *them*.]

We pray for [other] family and friends,
for the healing of their hurts
and the acceptance of new realities.

All this we ask in the name of the One
who sets us free from slavery to the past
and makes all things new,
even Jesus Christ our Savior. **Amen.**

The United Methodist Book of Worship

A Prayer for Wisdom

O Wisdom on High,
by you the meek are guided in judgment,
and light rises up in darkness for the godly.
Grant us, in all doubts and uncertainties,
the grace to ask what you would have us do,
that we may be saved from all false choices,
and that in your light we may see light,
and in your straight path may not stumble;
through Jesus Christ our Savior. Amen.

The Book of Common Prayer, alt.

A Prayer for Peaceable Conversations

Lord, make our hearts places of peace
and our minds harbors of tranquility.
Sow in our souls true love for you and for one another;
and root deeply within us friendship and unity,
and concord with reverence.
So may we give peace to each other sincerely
and receive it beautifully. Amen.

Native American

A Prayer for Tough Conversations

May the Spirit speak, and may we acknowledge her voice.
May we know when to abide in silence,
and when to give voice to the unexpressed.
May we come with hearts
prepared to share in vulnerability and trust.
May the peace of Christ be present
in the midst of uncertainty, fear, pain, and grief.
May our courage give birth to understanding, vision, and love.
Amen.

Kate Mackereth Fulton

A Prayer for After an Argument

God of restoration, healing, and wholeness,
your son Jesus tells us to forgive not seven times,
but seventy times seven.
Deliver us from hardness of heart.
Heal us from this tension.
Bring us closer together in spite of our tendency
to drive a wedge between ourselves.

Restore us to one another and to right relationship with you,
that our marriage (relationship) may reflect
the ever-yielding, ever-playful, ever-mutual love
of your Triune nature.
This, we pray, in the name of Jesus Christ,
who reconciles all things to himself,
he who lives and reigns with you and the Holy Spirit,
one God, forever and ever. Amen.

Nelson Cowan

A Prayer for Irreconcilable Differences

To be prayed by both parties:

Holy One, help us listen.
Still the noise around us and in us.
Still the urgency and anxiety.
Still the destruction, falsehood, and blame.

Break through with your still, small voice,
with your calm and clarity,
with your leading and light.

Time of silent confession

Holy One, help us listen
and help us move forward with hope and peace.
Amen.

Lisa Ann Moss Degrenia

A Prayer for Forgiveness

Author of love,
we are reluctant to set aside
our hurt, our anger, our disappointment.
Heal us with your tender touch,

that we might be cleansed of all unclean thoughts and actions,
freed from doubts that distract,
released from memories that constrict.
Forgive the sins done in our name, both the ones we know,
and the ones of which we are unaware.
Open our eyes to the power of your self-giving love
on the cross of your Son, Jesus Christ,
in whose name we pray. Amen.

Michael J. O'Donnell

A Prayer for a Friendship That Has Ended

God of Ruth and Naomi, of David and Jonathan,
God of beginnings and endings,
God of seasons, of moments, of transitions;
guide my faithful response to the ending of this friendship.
If I am to lament, help me to lament boldly.
If I am to shake the dust off my feet,
help me to do so courageously.
If I am to make amends, help me to discern your timing.
Help me to trust in you, as I take this one day at a time.
For the feelings named, and for the feelings left unprocessed,
I thank you for knowing me and loving me.
Through Jesus Christ, our faithful friend,
who lives and reigns with you and the Holy Spirit,
one God, forever and ever.
Amen.

Nelson Cowan

Healing and Wholeness

A Service of Healing

This service may be used in private or in corporate worship. It may take place in a church, home, or hospital, or at a meeting of a prayer group. The service may be adapted for special needs by selecting appropriate portions from it and from any of the additional resources.

GREETING AND PREPARATION

Bless the Lord, O my soul!
And all that is within me, bless God's holy name!
Bless the Lord, O my soul, and forget not all God's benefits.
The Lord forgives all our iniquity, and heals all our diseases.

We gather in the name of Jesus Christ,
whose ministry of transformative grace and healing love
is available to us today.
Let all who seek healing and wholeness
open their hearts to the Spirit of the Lord.

SCRIPTURE

Suggested lessons. Comments on the lesson(s) may be added as appropriate.

Psalm 13—A prayer of pain and sorrow.
Psalm 23—You have anointed my head with oil.
Psalm 42—My soul longs for you.
Psalm 121—I lift up my eyes to the hills.
Psalm 139—The inescapable God.
Psalm 146—God lifts the bowed down.
Ecclesiastes 3:1-11a—For everything there is a season.
Isaiah 40:28-31—The weak shall renew their strength.
Isaiah 43:1-3a, 18-19, 25—When you pass through the waters.

Isaiah 53:3-5—With his stripes we are healed.

Isaiah 61:1-3a—Good tidings to the afflicted.

Matthew 5:1-12—Blessed are they.

Matthew 11:28-30—All who labor and are heavy laden.

Matthew 15:21-28—The Canaanite woman's faith.

Matthew 26:36-39—Not what I want, but what you want.

Mark 1:21-28—Jesus heals a man with an unclean spirit.

Mark 6:7-13—Anointing of the sick with oil.

Mark 6:53-56—People brought the sick to Jesus.

Mark 10:46-52—Take heart; rise, Jesus is calling you.

Luke 5:17-26—Take up your pallet and walk.

Luke 8:43-48—The woman with an issue of blood.

Luke 17:11-19—Thanksgiving for healing.

John 5:2-18—Do you want to be healed?

John 9—Healing of the man born blind.

Acts 3:1-10—Peter and John heal the lame man.

Acts 5:12-16—Healings in Jerusalem.

Romans 8—Nothing can separate us from God's love.

2 Corinthians 1:3-5—God comforts us in affliction.

Colossians 1:11-29—May you be strengthened with all power.

Hebrews 12:1-2—Jesus, the perfecter of our faith.

James 5:13-16—Is any among you sick?

1 John 4:16b-19—There is no fear in love.

1 John 5:13-15—The confidence we have in Christ.

Revelation 21:1-4—New heaven and new earth.

The Word of God for the people of God.
Thanks be to God.

CONFESSION

The following introductory words may be adapted in a manner fitting for the situation.

Name(s), when we confess our sins, the scriptures remind us that God, who is faithful and just, will cleanse us from all unrighteousness. During this time of confession, would you rather observe silence together or talk through what is on your mind?

After gauging their response(s), one of the following forms of confession may be offered. The first is an invitation to silent confession; the second is an invitation to a prayerful conversation.

Receive the Word of the Lord from the letter of James:
Are any among you sick?
They should call for the elders of the church
and have them pray over them,
anointing them with oil in the name of the Lord.
The prayer of faith will save the sick,
and the Lord will raise them up;
and anyone who has committed sins will be forgiven.
Therefore confess your sins to one another,
and pray for one another,
so that you may be healed. (James 5:14–16a)
In the stillness and presence of the Lord,
let us confess our sins.
Silence may be kept, after which the leader may offer the assurance of pardon.

The following conversational prompt or another suitable form may be offered:
Name, the Scriptures tell us to bear one another's burdens
and so fulfill the law of Christ.
As your *sister/brother/friend* in Christ, I ask you now,
are you at peace with God,
or is there anything in your life
that causes you to feel separated from God
and less than the full person God calls you to be?
There may be silence, reflection, or personal sharing, after which the leader may offer the assurance of pardon.

ASSURANCE OF PARDON

Leader to all
Receive the good news:
Christ died for us while we were yet sinners;
that proves God's love toward us.
In the name of Jesus Christ, we are forgiven.
Glory to God. Amen.

[HOLY COMMUNION]

A pastor may administer Holy Communion (see pages 23-29). If the leader is a lay person who is extending the table (i.e., bringing consecrated elements from a service of word and table), they may pray The Lord's Prayer together prior to receiving the bread and cup. When distributing the elements, appropriate words such as "The body of Christ, given for you," and "The blood of Christ, given for you" may be offered.

PRAYERS FOR HEALING AND WHOLENESS WITH ANOINTING AND/OR LAYING ON OF HANDS

If there is anointing with oil, a leader touches a thumb to the oil and makes the sign of the cross on the person's forehead, in silence or using these or similar words:
Name, I anoint you with oil
in the name of the Father, and of the Son,
and of the Holy Spirit
(in the name of the holy and triune God)
(in the name of Jesus, the Christ, your Savior and Healer)
[*for specified purpose*].

If there is laying on of hands, a leader, who may be joined by others, lays hands upon each person's head, in silence or using these or similar words:

125

Name, I (we) lay my (our) hands on you
in the name of the Father, and of the Son,
and of the Holy Spirit
(in the name of the holy and triune God)
(in the name of Jesus, the Christ, your Savior and Healer)
[*for specified purpose*].

PRAYERS OF INTERCESSION

One of the following prayers or another suitable prayer may be offered.

A General Prayer of Healing for a Variety of Uses
Almighty God, we pray that *Name* may be comforted
in their suffering and made whole.
When they are afraid, give them courage;
when they feel weak, grant them your strength;
when they are afflicted, afford them patience;
when they are lost, offer them hope;
when they are alone, move us to their side;
[when death comes, open your arms to receive them].
In the name of Jesus Christ we pray. Amen.

For the Sick
God of compassion, source of life and health:
strengthen and relieve your servant(s), *Name*,
and give your power of healing
to those who minister to their needs,
that those for whom our prayers are offered
may find help in weakness
and have confidence in your loving care;
through him who healed the sick
and is the physician of our souls,
even Jesus Christ our Lord. Amen.

For Persons with a Life-threatening Illness
Lord Jesus Christ,
we come to you sharing the suffering that you endured.
Grant us patience during this time,
that as we and *Name* live with pain,
disappointment, and frustration,
we may realize that suffering is a part of life,
a part of life that you know intimately.
Touch *Name* in *his/her/their* time of trial,
hold *him/her/them* tenderly in your loving arms,
and let *him/her/them* know you care.
Renew us in our spirits,
even when our bodies are not being renewed,
that we might be ever prepared to dwell in your eternal home,
through our faith in you, Lord Jesus,
who died and are alive for evermore. Amen.

For Persons in Coma or Unable to Communicate
Eternal God, you have known us before we were here
and will continue to know us after we are gone.
Touch *Name* with your grace and presence.
As you give your abiding care,
assure *him/her/them* of our love and presence.
Assure *him/her/them* that our communion together
remains secure,
And that your love for *him/her/them* is unfailing.
In Christ, who came to us, we pray. Amen.

THE LORD'S PRAYER (if not prayed earlier)

BLESSING

The grace of the Lord Jesus Christ,
and the love of God,
and the communion of the Holy Spirit
be with you all. **Amen.**

The United Methodist Book of Worship, adapted
The United Methodist Hymnal

A Prayer for One Who Knows They Will Never Be Fully Well Again

O God, I know that when I get back home
life is never going to be quite the same again.
I know that I will always have to take care;
and that I will have to go much slower;
and that I will not be able to make the efforts
that I used to make.
Help me to be glad that I am as I am,
and that I have got what I have.
I am still alive, and I can still work;
I can still move about;
I can still meet my friends and see the beauty of the world.
I can see now that I was living at far too fast a pace,
and at far too great a pressure.
So, help me from now on to accept life as it is,
and to make the best of it.
And help me to be sure that, if I go about it in the right way,
life is not finished, but that the best is yet to be.
Let me remember what Paul said:
I have learned, in whatever state I am, to be content.
(Philippians 4:11)

William Barclay

A Prayer for Living Fully in the Dying Days

Loving God,
I am so grateful for the life I have had.
I am grateful for the love I have received and given.
I am grateful for the strength I have found
to move forward through the years.
I am so grateful for the special people in my life:
Name, Name, and Name.

128

Loving God, give us the ability to live each of the final days
that we have together to the full.
May we do the things we want to do
even if they are risky and not what others expect.
May we say the words that are on our hearts
and lie deep within that deepest part of us,
and may we join with family and friends
in remembering, in laughter,
and in peacefully being together.
We want to make the earthly time we have together
a happy time,
a fulfilling time, and a time of great joy.
We know that you are with us as our wish comes true.
Bless every day, bless every minute of every day,
and bless every second of every minute of every day
we live and love and hope and struggle and share together.
Amen.

David Sparks and Sheila Noyes

A Prayer for the Courage to Move on from the Past

Lord, I commit my failures
as well as my successes
into your hands,
and I bring for your healing
the people and the situations,
the wrongs and the hurts of the past.
Give me courage, strength and generosity
to let go and move on,
leaving the past behind me,
and living the present to the full.

Lead me always to be positive
as I entrust the past to your mercy,
the present to your love,
and the future to your providence.

Attributed to St. Augustine of Hippo

A Prayer in Times of Worry

Heavenly Father,
you are indeed my Lord and God!
You made me out of nothing
and redeemed me through your Son.
You have commanded and appointed me
to perform my duties and labors,
which I, however, cannot accomplish as I desire,
and there are many troubles that frighten and oppress me,
so that I am, as to my own power,
without help and consolation;
therefore I commend all things into your hands.
Help and console me, and be my all in all.
Amen.

Attributed to Martin Luther

A Prayer for Those Who Mourn

Gracious God,
as your Son wept with Mary and Martha
at the tomb of Lazarus, look with compassion
on those who grieve [, especially *Name(s)*].
Grant them the assurance of your presence now
and faith in your eternal goodness,
that in them may be fulfilled the promise
that those who mourn shall be comforted;
through Jesus Christ our Lord. Amen.

The United Methodist Hymnal

A Prayer for the Loss of a Child

All-loving and caring God, Parent of us all, you know our grief in our loss, for you too suffered the death of your child. Give us strength to go forward from this day, trusting, where we do not understand, that your love never ends. When all else fails, you still are God. We thank you for the life and hope that you give through the resurrection of your Son Jesus Christ. We pray to you for one another in our need, and for all, anywhere, who mourn with us this day. To those who doubt, give light; to those who are weak, strength; to all who have sinned, mercy; to all who sorrow, your peace. Keep true in us the love with which we hold one another. And to you, with your Church on earth and in heaven, we offer honor and praise, now and forever. Amen.

The United Methodist Book of Worship

A Prayer on the Death Anniversary of a Loved One

Or during any time of grief over the loss of a loved one

When the wall
between the worlds
is too firm,
too close.

When it seems
all solidity
and sharp edges.

When every morning
you wake as if
flattened against it,

its forbidding presence
fairly pressing the breath
from you
all over again.

Then may you be given
a glimpse
of how weak the wall

and how strong what stirs
on the other side,

breathing with you
and blessing you
still

forever bound to you
but freeing you
into this living,
into this world
so much wider
than you ever knew.

Jan Richardson

A Prayer for Those Addicted to Drugs

Lord, we are praying for those we love
whose lives are chained by the power of drugs.
They have sacrificed everything to this cruel master:
work, home, relationships, honesty,
even love seems barely to matter.
And still more is demanded of them:
we fear it will take their very life.
We need a miracle
because we've done everything we can think of.

Where there is recklessness, bring caution,
where there is compulsion, bring freedom,
where there is desperation, bring hope,
where death looms,
we need your power to save.
You broke the power of the grave,
you can rescue this dear one.
Thank you that your gaze is on us continually,
even those lost in the maze of addiction
are dear to you, you call them by name.
Nothing can stop your love.
Give us strength to walk this journey faithfully.
You walk with us,
the journey is long.

Carol Penner

A Service for the Loss of a Beloved Pet

This service is most suitable for taking place inside someone's home, or at a burial site for the beloved pet.

OPENING WORDS

I lift up my eyes to the hills:
from where will my help come?
My help comes from the Lord:
who made heaven and earth. (Psalm 121:1-2 NRSVUE)

CANTICLE

Let the earth glorify the Lord,
sing praise and give honor for ever.
Glorify the Lord, O mountains and hills,
and all that grows upon the earth,
sing praise and give honor for ever.
Glorify the Lord, O springs of water, seas, and streams,
O whales and all that move in the waters.

All birds of the air, glorify the Lord,
sing praise and give honor for ever.
Glorify the Lord, O beasts of the wild,
and all you, cats and dogs, flocks and herds.
O people everywhere, glorify the Lord,
sing praise and give honor for ever.
Amen.

Canticle 12

SCRIPTURE READING

"But ask the animals what they think—let them teach you;
let the birds tell you what's going on. Put your ear to the
earth—learn the basics. Listen—the fish in the ocean will
tell you their stories. Isn't it clear that they all know and
agree that GOD is sovereign, that he holds all things in his
hand—Every living soul, yes, every breathing creature?"
(Job 12:7-10 The Message)

The word of God for the people of God.
Thanks be to God.

WITNESS

All are invited to share favorite moments, stories, memories.

BURIAL / SCATTERING OF ASHES (OPTIONAL)

We return *N.'s* remains to the earth with gratitude for your
care for us and for all that you have made. Your mercy is
over all your works, Father, Son, and Holy Spirit, now and
for ever. Amen.

COMMENDATION

One: The Lord be with you
ALL: And also with you

One: Let us pray. God of grace and glory, we remember before you today our beloved companion, *N.* We thank you for giving *N.* to us to be a source of abundant love, affection, and joy. In your compassion, comfort us who grieve. Give us faith to commit this beloved creature of your own making to your care, for you live and reign for ever and ever. Amen.

The Journal of the General Convention
of The Episcopal Church, adapted

Leadership and Church Life

A Prayer of Commissioning for Missionaries or a Mission Team

Blessed God, you call forth light from darkness: Send the power of your Spirit upon your servants *N. (and N.)* as they carry your Gospel to_____. May your light so fill them that they may shine with your radiance, drawing all to the brightness of your love and mercy; through Jesus, our Savior and true Light. Amen.

The Book of Occasional Services, The Episcopal Church

A Prayer for the Consecration of a Building, or Celebration of a Remodel

God of love, you are our home, our shelter,
and the place of our belonging.
We give thanks for this space,
and all those who have prepared it.
May it be a place of worship and service
for all who enter it.

135

May it be a place of beauty and joy,
a place of belonging and healing.
God, as these walls enclose us,
may your grace surround us.
May your love uphold us,
the doors of your grace open to us new possibilities,
the windows of your wisdom open our eyes
to see the world through your love.
God, bless this space, and bless all who enter it.
And may we ourselves be your building,
the home of your love,
that our lives may offer welcome and grace
to all who draw near. Amen.

Steve Garnaas-Holmes

A Prayer for Church Discernment

God of grace and mystery, you call us.
Like young Samuel in the temple
we do not know your call clearly
without each other's help.
Guide us as we face a decision together.
Give us humility to learn from others,
and to go the journey together
as needed companions.
Give us the heart of Christ to risk for the sake of others,
and the tongues of the Spirit to trust each other's wisdom.
Give us silence to listen, space to hear,
grace to accept, and courage to dare.
Give us the faith to follow the calling we discern.
Above all give us love,
that all we do and say, all we think and hear,

we may do so with your love for one another,
for you, and for the world you call us to serve.
Speak, God, for your servants are listening. Amen.

Steve Garnaas-Holmes

A Covenant to Precede Difficult Conversations

We gather around the table acknowledging God's unbounded grace for all. We come from different backgrounds, and we acknowledge our differences of opinion and perspectives on many matters. Yet we gather still, knowing that Jesus calls us to break bread and share the cup no matter what, and that each of us has a place here.

And so, as we gather around the table we commit to:

1. Stay curious. We come with a willingness to learn and commit to staying at the table. When the going gets rough, we will turn to wonder, ask questions, and stay engaged.

2. Be kind. There will be statements shared at the table that will challenge our perspectives. We will be respectful in our responses and engagement, treating each one with grace and love.

3. Listen with the same amount of passion with which we want to be heard. In the words of St. Francis, we will seek to understand more than to be understood. We also commit to share the air and not dominate.

Do you affirm this covenant together? If so, let us say "we do."
We do.

Marcia McFee

A Prayer during Change

Almighty God, change is bittersweet. In order to change we are forced both to leave something behind and to embrace something new. Grant us the grace on this day to do both with humility. Help us affirm the good things of our past as we lean into a future where there will also be good things. As we contemplate the changes that will come, remind us that all good things come from You. Today we commit ourselves to the necessary work ahead. Be present with us, work in us and through us, we pray. Amen.

Safiyah Fosua

A Prayer for Those Leaving Our Church

When anyone leaves our church family,
we are never quite the same.
Today we say farewell to *N. [and N.]*.
It is with sadness that we see him/her/them go,
yet we acknowledge that God may call
any of us in new directions.
For *(number)* years, you have been part of this congregation.
Your strengths and needs have joined our strengths and needs.
We have shared worship, hard work,
fellowship, and growth in the faith.
You have given of your time, your energy, and your gifts.
As you leave us, we pray that you will continue
to be faithful to God's call.
Remember us as friends and co-workers in Christ.
Support us with your continuing love and prayers,
even as we will support you.

Peter Wyatt

A Collect for The United Methodist Church

God of the Ages, who called Abraham and Sarah to journey to a land that you promised:
Guide the people called United Methodist through our current distress to a place of peace and rekindled vision, that we may yet participate in the transformation of the world, and that our neighbors may find in us generous friends; through Jesus Christ, the Good Shepherd, who with you and the Holy Spirit, lives and reigns, one God, now and forever. Amen.

Mark W. Stamm

A Prayer for Those Who Find Themselves without a Church

This prayer is intended for use in the wake of a disaffiliation and/or church split.

God of desert and wilderness,
who draws near to us in our wandering,
sustain us now in the unexpected journey
of being without a church home.
Steady us so that we are present
to all you may offer us during this in-between moment.
Work for the healing of our hearts.
Help us grapple with the jarring separation from friends—
people with whom we have prayed, worshiped, and served—
co-laborers in your kingdom.
Deliver us from any mean-spiritedness that lingers,
and lead us to pray for them daily.
In your tender care, guide us in our next steps.

We place our hope and trust in you,
confident that you will bring us to the place
you have prepared.
Through Jesus Christ, our Lord.
Amen.

Nelson Cowan

A Prayer for Pastoral Leadership during Holy Week

Faithful and loving God, this week is both an emotional rollercoaster and a labor of love. Our pastoral duties collide with our personal faith journeys, as well as with memories of Holy Weeks in years past, celebrated with spouses, friends, and family members who may no longer be with us. Remind us of your steadfastness in the midst of our swirling thoughts, de-centered spirits, and unfettered fears. Enable us to linger in the checkered nostalgia of Maundy Thursday, the wrenching pain of Good Friday, and the disquieting silence of Holy Saturday. Upon doing so, equip us then to celebrate with resounding joy the good news of your Son's resurrection for the life of the world. It is in his name we pray—he who lives and reigns with you and the Holy Spirit, one God, now and forever. Amen.

Nelson Cowan

A Prayer for Those
with Imposter Syndrome

God of reminders and gentle nudging,
I know I'm competent and called, and that you have
equipped me for all that is before me. I know this well. And
yet, I still doubt my abilities. I compare. I contrast. I draw
lines in the sand. Remind me of your faithfulness that I've
witnessed. Instill within me what I already know, but often
refuse to believe: that I am yours—beloved and known. I ask
this in the name of Jesus, who lives and reigns with you and
the Holy Spirit, one God, now and forever. Amen.

Nelson Cowan

A Prayer for Singing

We are people who must sing you,
for the sake of our very lives.
You are a God who must be sung by us,
for the sake of your majesty and honor.
And so we thank you,
for lyrics that push us past our reasons,
for melodies that break open our givens,
for cadences that locate us home,
beyond all our safe places,
for tones and tunes that open our lives beyond control
and our futures beyond despair.
We thank you for the long parade of mothers and fathers
who have sung you deep and true;
We thank you for the good company
of artists, poets, musicians, cantors, and instruments
that sing for us and with us, toward you.
We are witnesses to your mercy and splendor;
We will not keep silent . . . ever again. Amen.

Walter Brueggemann

A Prayer before a Budget Meeting

Faithful One,
to whom all things belong,
and in whom all things find their worth.
Your son Jesus teaches us
to be faithful and wise managers of your resources.
Give us your wisdom as we seek
to allocate these resources responsibly.
Lead us to align our financial aims
with the priorities of your kingdom.
Temper any worries we might have
through the nurturing presence of your Holy Spirit.
This, we pray, through Jesus Christ, our Lord.
Amen.

Nelson Cowan

A Prayer for Quilting Groups

God of creation and beauty,
You knit us together in our mother's womb,
pieced us together with skill and care,
and continue to craft us more and more
into the image of your Son.
You have unrolled your grace upon us,
not by the inch or yard, but bolt over bolt.
In every stitch and punch, appliqué and mount,
you have been faithful.
Through our work together,
you have taken our individual identities
and quilted us into a community.

As we prepare to [*begin our work / leave this place*],
give us hearts wadded with memories,
lives bordered with gratitude,
and let the ties that bind us together now
be but the beginning of what is yet to come.
In the name of Jesus, in whom all things hold together,
we pray.
Amen.

Drew Weseman

A Prayer for the Ending
of a Longtime Church Ministry

God of seasons and life rhythms, as we celebrate the life of this ministry, help us to know how valuable and sacred it is to have a place to belong. We give thanks for all the faithful servants who [*insert activities here*], and gave selflessly of their time and talents to create and sustain [*ministry name*]. We ask, O God, that [*ministry name*]'s legacy of [*its purpose*] would continue to be a part of our church's DNA. Help us who carry on to draw strength, encouragement, and ingenuity from the examples of this ministry and its many seasoned saints. Bless them for all they have done, and for all that their past work and witness will continue to do in the days and years to come. In the name of the One who sustains us, we pray. Amen.

Kate Mackereth Fulton

Family and Home

A Prayer before Baking Bread

God of the harvest, as grains of wheat, once scattered across the fields, have been gathered here in this kitchen, let my mixing, kneading, folding, and shaping be an extension of your creative and unifying work. As I wait for the dough to proof and rise, let your attentive patience increase within me, so that I may move at the pace of your Kingdom as it spreads throughout our world. And as the warm aroma of nearly baked bread wafts from my oven and fills the house with anticipation, let my love for you send me out of my home to welcome friends and strangers to join us as we feast over broken loaves in a community of grace.

Drew Weseman

A Prayer before Preparing a Meal

As I hold ingredients that need to be prepared,
thank you for the ground from which they came.
As I set a table to welcome family, [friends, strangers,]
thank you for the community we will form
through your Spirit.
As I pause before this meal I am privileged to prepare,
thank you for allowing me to participate
in your creative work.
In my cooking, cleaning, and eating,
let me experience your grace
so that I may share it with all who will soon gather here.
Amen.

Drew Weseman

A Prayer for Enjoying Wine

NOTE: Historically, many Methodists have advocated for abstinence from some or all forms of alcohol, so this prayer may not be fitting for your setting.

Blessed are you, O Lord our God, creator of the fruit of the vine: Grant that we who share this wine, which gladdens our hearts, may share forever the new life of the true Vine, your Son Jesus Christ our Lord. Amen.

The Book of Occasional Services, The Episcopal Church

Table Blessings

A.

This prayer could be done responsively, with one person leading, and others responding "thank you Lord."

For this food, thank you Lord
For [N.] who prepared it, thank you Lord
For those who produced it, thank you Lord
And to you who created everything we need, thank you Lord. Amen.

Traditional, Author Unknown

B.

Sung to OLD ONE HUNDREDTH (Praise God from whom all blessings flow)

Be present at our table, Lord;
be here and everywhere adored;
thy creatures bless, and grant that we
may feast in paradise with thee. Amen.

The United Methodist Hymnal

C.

Blessed are you, O Lord God, Ruler of the Universe,
for you give us food to sustain our lives
and make our hearts glad;
through Jesus Christ our Lord. Amen.

The Book of Common Prayer, adapted

D.

God, to those who have hunger, give bread.
And to those who have bread, give the hunger for justice.
Amen.

Presbyterian Mission Agency, Latin America

E.

Come Lord Jesus, be our guest,
let this food to us be blessed. Amen.

Traditional Lutheran

F.

For food in a world where many are in hunger;
for faith in a world where many are in fear;
for friends in a world where many are alone,
We give you humble thanks, O Lord.

The World Hunger Grace, Author Unknown

A Brief Prayer of Blessing of a Home

Bless and sanctify with your peace, O God, this home and
those who live in it, that within these walls they may know
the blessings of this life and to know the promise of the life
to come in that heavenly home, where with saints and angels
you live and reign, one God forever and ever. Amen.

The Book of Occasional Services, The Episcopal Church

A Prayer for [a] New Parent[s]

God of the humble and hopeful,
you bless those who believe when you promise.
Help us, like Mary and Elizabeth,
simply to delight in the good things
you prepare for us,
to say "yes,"
and to trust that your strength and your love
will provide the wisdom needed by those
who care for *N.*
Amen.

A New Zealand Prayer Book – He Karakia Mihinare o Aotearoa

A Blessing for an Adoption

Friends, we have all been adopted into God's family
by the will and grace of Jesus
Christ, so we give thanks for this adoption
of [*child name(s)*] into this family.

Let us pray:

Gracious God, bless [*child name(s)*] with wisdom,
understanding, peace, and the assurance of your love
for them now and forever.
Guide and protect them throughout their life journeys,
and bless them always with the
knowledge of [*parent(s) name(s)*] love for them.
We also ask your blessing upon [*parent(s) name(s)*].
Give them strength to love, nurture,
and care for [*this/these child(ren)*] being adopted.
Nurture these parents [*this parent*]
with the love and gentleness that only you can bring.

Bless their home with your presence,
that their family would be nourished
by your Word, and their lives accompanied by your Spirit.
We ask all of this in the name
of our adopted sibling and Savior,
Jesus the Christ who reigns with you and the Holy Spirit,
One God, forever and ever. Amen.

Angela Rotherham

A Prayer for Help to Conceive or to Accept Infertility

Merciful Creator, every day you bring new life into this
world. We long to share in this generation by bearing a
child. Yet our attempts have brought grief, frustration, and
fear. Now we feel spent and our hope fades. Give us grace
to surrender our longing to you. Hold our hearts' desire in
your heart, helping us trust that our lives unfold according
to your unfailing love, through Christ our Redeemer. Amen.

Enriching Our Worship 5: Liturgies and Prayers
Related to Childbearing, Childbirth, and Loss

A Prayer for Letting Go the Hope of Childbearing

Holy God, you offer abundance of life and fullness of joy
to your children. We have longed to bear children of our
own. As we grieve the loss of this dream, turn our sorrow to
hope for a different future than the one we had imagined.
Transform the desires of our hearts into grace that we may
bear your love to others in all we do and say, through Jesus
Christ, our Redeemer. Amen.

Enriching Our Worship 5: Liturgies and Prayers
Related to Childbearing, Childbirth, and Loss

Prayers of the Saints

A Prayer of Saint Patrick

Christ be with us, Christ before us, Christ behind us,
Christ in us, Christ beneath us, Christ above us,
Christ on our right, Christ on our left,
Christ where we lie, Christ where we sit,
Christ where we arise,
Christ in the heart of every one who thinks of us,
Christ in every eye that sees us,
Christ in every ear that hears us.
Salvation is of the Lord,
Salvation is of the Christ,
May your salvation, O Lord, be ever with us.

Saint Patrick

A Prayer of Susanna Wesley

You, O Lord, have called us to watch and pray.
Therefore, whatever may be the sin against which we pray,
make us careful to watch against it,
and so have reason to expect that our prayers will be answered.
In order to perform this duty aright,
grant us grace to preserve a sober, equal temper,
and sincerity to pray for your assistance. Amen.

Susanna Wesley

A Prayer of St. Francis of Assisi

Lord, make me an instrument of thy peace;
where there is hatred, let me sow love;
where there is injury, pardon;
where there is doubt, faith;
where there is despair, hope;
where there is darkness, light;
and where there is sadness, joy.
O Divine Master,
grant that I may not so much seek
to be consoled as to console;
to be understood, as to understand;
to be loved, as to love;
for it is in giving that we receive,
it is in pardoning that we are pardoned,
and it is in dying that we are born to eternal life.
Attributed to St. Francis of Assisi, The United Methodist Hymnal

Labor, Vocation, Hobbies

A Prayer for Today

Today is the day, Lord.
If the heavens can stretch its arms
wide enough to hold all the worlds you have made,
then so can I—today is the day.
If the sun can bring warmth and beauty
to both the meadow and the trash heap,
then so can I—today is the day.
If the leaves can so easily change and
find their purpose with each season,
then so can I—today is the day.
If the birds can never grow weary of
singing their songs even in the cold of winter,
then so can I—today is the day.

If the ants can never stop building and
fighting for the common good,
then so can I—today is the day.
If the groundhog can periodically stop
to rest deeply in your provision and protection,
then so can I—today is the day.
If the infant can still so easily delight in others
who may or may not have their best interests in mind,
then so can I—today is the day.
Today is the day, Lord,
for me to be renewed and re-created by your grace,
till the splendor of your image is made clear
in my being,
my doing,
my speaking,
my waiting,
my resting. Amen.

R. DeAndre Johnson

A Prayer of Discernment for an Individual

God, my Source of Strength:
a season is turning in my life
calling me to make ready:
walk with me, I pray.
This unmapped course lies divided ahead,
urging careful determination:
walk with me, I pray.
The gate has swung open and everything's loose,
bidding that something be left behind:
walk with me, I pray.
Until the turbulent waters clear,
I reach for your mercy and pray for wisdom:
walk with me, I pray.
Amen.

Keri K. Wehlander

A Prayer When Work Is Scarce

Abba, I've heard it said, Your children don't beg for bread (Psalm 37:25), but my hand is outstretched and nearly empty. I can hardly provide for my family. I struggle to make ends meet. We live paycheck to paycheck. I work with no satisfaction and little reward, with the growing anxiety of needing to provide. You hold it all, Jesus. Yes, even this. You hold it all.

Abba, As I apply for job after job, hoping for an interview or a phone call, I bring to you my despair. I bring to you my own feelings of worthlessness and inadequacy. I bring to you the fear and the worry that consume my thoughts by day and make my soul restless at night. You hold it all, Jesus. Yes, even this. You hold it all.

Abba, I grow bitter at the ease and comfort others around me experience. Do they not recognize the blessing of their own security? Do they not understand the gift of having enough? Why do some have plenty while others go without? Certainly, you are a God of abundance so help me believe what I cannot see. Help me embrace the substance of hope. You hold it all, Jesus. Yes, even this. You hold it all.

Abba, Help me find the place—the space between the paradox of your provision and my need for work. Circumstance and the enemy's lies won't bury my resolve. At the end of the day, may I proclaim: "May the favor of the Lord our God rest on us; establish the work of our hands for us—yes, establish the work of our hands" (Psalm 90:17 [NIV]). You hold it all, Jesus. Yes, even this. You hold it all. In Jesus' Name. Amen.

Andrea Hunter and Katie Ritsema-Roelofs

A Blessing for Active Military Leaving for Deployment

God of Love and Compassion,

We have come to ask for your protection for those who are being sent to faraway places to prepare for our defense. Before this season of unrest, we had grown comfortable with thinking of them only as they relate to us—as our parents and spouses, our sons and daughters, our neighbors and friends. We look forward to a day when no community will ever be asked to release its loved ones for purposes of war. But today, Lord, history and circumstances force us to release them into your care and into our country's service. We pray for their safe return; and not only for theirs, but for the safe return of others who are being sent from communities, so much like ours, in other parts of the world. As they face the myriad challenges and decisions that each day is destined to bring, may they be anchored by their faith, protected by your presence, and comforted by the knowledge that they are loved by you and by this community.

We bless them in your name, and look forward to their safe return, through Jesus Christ our Lord. Amen.

Safiyah Fosua

A Prayer for Caregivers

God, our refuge and strength, our present help in time of trouble, care for those who tend the needs of [*the sick*]/ [*name/s*]. Strengthen them in body and spirit. Refresh them when weary; console them when anxious; comfort them in grief; and hearten them in discouragement. Be with us all, and give us peace at all times and in every way; through Christ our peace. Amen.

Evangelical Lutheran Worship

A Prayer for Health Care Providers

Merciful God, your healing power is everywhere about us.
Strengthen those who work among the sick; give them courage and confidence in all they do. Encourage them when their efforts seem futile or when death prevails. Increase their trust in your power even to overcome death and pain and crying. May they be thankful for every sign of health you give, and humble before the mystery of your healing grace; through Jesus Christ our Lord. Amen.

Evangelical Lutheran Worship

A Prayer for First Responders

Blessed are you, Lord, God of mercy,
who through your Son gave us a marvelous example of charity
and the great commandment of love for one another.
Send down your blessings on these your servants,
who so generously devote themselves to helping others.
When they are called on in times of need,
let them faithfully serve you in their neighbor.
We ask this through Christ our Lord. R. Amen.

The Book of Blessings

A Blessing for Educational Institutions

O Eternal God, bless all schools, colleges, and universities
(*especially . . .*),
that they may be lively centers for sound learning,
new discovery and the pursuit of wisdom;
grant that those who teach
and those who learn
may find you to be the source of all truth.
We make this prayer through Jesus Christ. Amen.

A New Zealand Prayer Book – He Karakia Mihinare o Aotearoa

A Blessing for a Time of Sabbatical

NOTE: it is best to ask the person preparing for sabbatical to bring their own cell phone and computer. This can be done with one leader or two.

Leader 1: I invite *N.* to come forward at this time, that this community might send you forth with our love as you approach your time of sabbatical.

Leader 2: *N.*, we begin by setting aside for sacred purpose these computers and these cell phones, a sign of the work that fills your time while you are with us. Anticipating your sabbatical season, we ask God's blessing on these tools, *Leaders 1 and 2 here touch the cell phone and computer.* that you may use them lightly in the coming months, so that your time of rest may be full and deep, and you may attend even more closely to God, your own spirits, and the family and friends who are dearest to you. *Name*, will you receive this blessing of freedom in the months to come? If so, say, "I do."

[I do.]

Leader 1: Let us pray. Grace-filled God, we thank you for your servant, *N.* We praise you for their love and care for your church and your world, lived out in ministry among us. Now we pray, Gentle Shepherd, that you will lead them beside still waters and make them lie down in green pastures. Restore their souls to your glory, Great God. Set before them a table of grace. Grant travel mercies and bring them home safely to us. And now, Holy One, look with wisdom and love on us all gathered here, that even in the rush of our daily work we may seek your presence and know the peace that passes all understanding through the grace of Jesus Christ. Amen.

Ruth Duck

A Prayer for Artists and Musicians

O God,
whom saints and angels delight to worship in heaven:
Be ever present with your servants
who seek through art and music
to perfect the praises
offered by your people on earth;
and grant to them even now glimpses of your beauty,
and make them worthy at length to behold it
unveiled forevermore;
through Jesus Christ our Lord. Amen.

The Book of Common Prayer

A Prayer to Appreciate Pauses in Life

O Christ who draws playfully in the sand,
teach me to value the pauses in my life.
Remind me that not everything
needs a purpose or demands results.
Give me the capacity to delight in what is before me—
not worrying, not rushing . . . just trusting, somehow.
In your matchless name, I pray.
Amen.

Nelson Cowan

A Prayer for Engaging a Prayer Labyrinth

Almighty God, to you all hearts are open,
all desires known, and from you no secrets are hidden.
You set the foundations of the earth
and the boundaries of the sea.
Guide now our feet, our hearts, and our minds
to love and serve you always.

Let each footfall or movement forward
be a new connection to you and your love,
Creator, Redeemer, and Friend.
Give us strength and grace with each course of this Labyrinth,
that by our walking or wheeling or tracing with fingers
we may dance in praise of you,
and perceive with joy the angelic rhythm
unseen or unheard, except in the hearts of believers;
through Christ our Lord. Amen.

Robert Elsner

A Prayer for a Garden

God of Creation, all the earth is yours,
and all that is in it.
You have created this soil,
brought forth living things,
and nourished them with sun and rain.
Bless now this garden
as a source of joy and beauty.
Hidden in the soil
is the work of death and resurrection.
May it bear fruit in the lives of your beloved
with nourishment and beauty,
with joy and gratitude, with peace and rest.
May all creatures, great and small,
who draw near receive your blessing here.
As living things sprout and grow forth from this soil—
"the earth produces of itself, the sower knows not how"—
may your grace grow and bear fruit in us.
Bless this garden, and all who cherish it,
that it may be a sign for us
of your beautiful, miraculous, life-giving love. Amen.

Steve Garnaas-Holmes

A Prayer for Travel

Sojourning God,
your Spirit exists everywhere, on every path,
inviting us to move with curiosity and compassion.
Give us courage as we leave the familiar,
venturing out beyond our walls,
taking leave so that we will see with wider vision,
know with deeper appreciation,
and exist with expanded perception.
Nudge us, guide us,
and keep us safe, we pray.
Amen.

Marcia McFee

A Prayer for Going on Vacation

O Lord, you who promise to be with us in our coming and
our going, we ask your blessing upon us as we begin this
vacation; help us to release to you all that we leave behind:
the people that we love, the pressures that weary us, the tasks
that we left unfinished and the problems that would hound
and haunt us; help us also to embrace all that you would
have for us: the joy of adventure, the delight of companionship, the laughter of play, the rest of soul and the discovery
of beauty; and may we be refreshed in our going and replen-
ished in our coming. We pray this in the name of the One
who delights to give his children good gifts. Amen.

W. David O. Taylor

158

Affirmation and Inclusion

A Blessing for Someone Who Embodies a New Name

NOTE: Methodists have diverse theological perspectives concerning gender and sexuality, so this prayer may not be fitting for your setting.

This prayer uses the pronouns "they/them." After consulting with the person being blessed, please use the pronouns they prefer.

Loving God, in renaming your servants
Abraham, Sarah, Jacob, Peter, and Paul,
you gave them new lives and new tasks,
new love, and new hope.
We now hold before you our companion *N.*
Bless *them* with a new measure of grace
as *they* take this new name.
Hold *them* in your heart, written on your palm,
And grant that we may all be held in your presence,
for the sake of Christ whose name is Love,
in whom, with you and the Spirit, we pray. Amen.

[optional sending blessing that may be adapted for this prayer, or the gender transition prayer below]

N., we know you now by your true name [*and gender*].
Bear this name in the Name of Christ,
and may the Holy Spirit,
who has begun a good work in you,
direct and uphold you in the service
of Christ and his Kingdom;
in the name of the Holy and Undivided Trinity.
[in the name of the Father, and of the Son,
and the Holy Spirit.]
Amen.

*Pastoral Liturgies for Journeys of Gender Affirmation
and Transition Rites and Prayers Supplemental to The Book
of Alternative Services of The Anglican Church of Canada*

A Prayer of Affirmation for Gender Transition

NOTE: *Methodists have diverse theological perspectives concerning gender and sexuality, so this prayer may not be fitting for your setting.*

This prayer uses the pronouns "they/them." After consulting with the person being blessed, please use the pronouns they prefer.

God our provider, you loved us into birth,
and even more love us through the changes of our life.
We pray for our friend, *N.*, who this day stands with us
in your presence seeking blessing
on the transition *they* are beginning [*or have begun*].
To those who persevere in faith, you show us wonders,
O Holy One, and we delight as the mystery
of *N.'s* self is revealed in these new ways.
Give *them* courage and deep compassion for self and others
throughout the challenges in the times ahead,
and open *their* mouth anew to proclaim your praise. Amen.

Pastoral Liturgies for Journeys of Gender Affirmation and
Transition Rites and Prayers Supplemental to The Book
of Alternative Services of The Anglican Church of Canada

A Prayer for Finding Beauty within Ourselves

Dearest loving beautiful God, Creator of all;
We give thanks for the allure and attractiveness
of every single one of us.
We are created in your image,
created in beauty and power and promise.
Help us to recognize with our minds,
and our hearts,
and our spirits,
what is truly gorgeous and glorious.

Open us to respond to the inner beauty that resides within,
resisting the myths of our superficial culture.
May we find within ourselves, confidence in our being.
May we understand that cosmetics do not define normalcy,
that aesthetics are an addition and not the core of who we are.
Help us, O God, to find beauty within ourselves.
Liberate us from the norms of what is desirable and attractive.
Shallow standards hold us captive,
by limiting imagination and connection
by reinforcing contemptible stereotypes and
detracting from our collective humanity.
Release us from the prisons of preference and privilege
that condemn through physical appearance.
Let us love ourselves so that we may love our neighbors.
Attune us to all the forms of beauty in this wonderful world,
within and around us,
may we be your beloved and beautiful people.
In Christ, we pray,
Amen.

Kenji Marui

A Prayer for the World and Its Peoples

O God, you are the hope of all the ends of the earth,
the God of the spirits of all flesh.
Hear our humble intercession
for all races and families on earth,
that you will turn all hearts to yourself.
Remove from our minds hatred, prejudice, and contempt,
for those who are not of our own race or color, class or creed,
that, departing from everything that estranges and divides,
we may by you be brought into unity of spirit,
in the bond of peace. Amen.

Church of Scotland, 20th Cent, alt.

A Prayer of Thanksgiving for All

Holy One, we thank you for the gift of life
in its vast arrays and complexities.
We thank you for the gift of friendship.
Jesus, we thank you that you modeled
a life of service and compassion
to the people whom society often forgot or ignored.
Wise Spirit, we need your loving eyes
in order to care for those you have put in our midst.
We need greater grace in order to serve
and be in ministry with everyone.
We ask all of this, so that more people
can become part of the great story
of your love in action. This is why we pray,
Thy Kingdom Come. Amen.

Amanda Larsen, adapted with permission from Scott Roberts

A Prayer of Welcome
after an Absence from Church

Blessed are you, Lord our God, you watch over our going
out, and our coming in. Our beloved, *N.*, has returned to us
from _____. We thank you for being our companion on
the way, for bringing us together in this community, and for
sealing us in your covenant of love. Guide us in our pilgrim-
age until we find our home with you that, strengthened by
your love, we may live in the bond of peace. We ask it for the
sake of Jesus Christ. Amen.

The Book of Occasional Services, The Episcopal Church

A Blessing for Someone
Who Should Not Need to Be Resilient

Come, you who are exhausted by the need to be resilient.
Let God give you rest.
Come, you who are burdened by traditions and systems,
expectations and oppression.
Let God loose the yoke.
Come, lay at the altar all that's been laid upon you.
Though you are strong, it's too heavy to carry.
Though you are strong, remember that Christ
is the only solid rock.
Come, be held.
Be still and truly know that God is still God.
Though your earth shakes;
though your hopes crumble and fall into the sea;
though war rages around you,
within you—you may lay down your weapons,
and you may trust that even in weakness
(especially in weakness),
you are made strong.
Strong enough for stillness. Strong enough for trust.

May the peace that passes all understanding never pass you by.
May joy come even sooner than the morning—
for you have wept enough nights.
May you meet God over and over again—
as provider and protector,
as warrior and friend.
May you know God—not as a far away, untouchable idea,
like justice or equity.
May you know the true presence of God—
intimately, internally, eternally.

Weary ones, strong ones,
those exhausted by the need to be resilient—
may you be blessed with occasional ease
that frees you from the need for resilience.
May you be blessed with rest and restoration, even now.
May it be so.
Amen.

Eleanor Colvin

Justice and Peace

An Interfaith Prayer for Justice

Spirit of Life and Love, dear God of all nations: There is so much work to do. We have only begun to imagine justice and mercy.

Help us hold fast to our vision of what can be. May we see the hope in our history, and find the courage and the voice to work for that constant rebirth of freedom and justice. That is our dream. Amen.

William Sinkford

A Prayer before Attending a Demonstration

In the Name of the God of Peace, the Nonviolent Christ, and the Liberating Spirit, Amen.

God of Peace, as I prepare to participate in this demonstration, stir up in me the gifts I need to cooperate with you in establishing the beloved community, here and now. Through the witness of my brother, Jesus, may I incarnate the grace of nonviolence which calls me to envision a wider circle of authentic welcome. May I never shy away from my prophetic vocation by declaring your radical truth of justice, even when it is inconvenient to my career, unpopular to my social circles, or disturbing to those in power. By the power of the Liberating Spirit, may I always step forward into the fray and birth the solidarity that will save this world. In the name of all that is good, holy, and beautiful, Amen.

Jerry Maynard (The People's Priest), Episcopal Street Action Handbook

A Prayer for the Lips of Prophets

For those weary of sharing their pain.
For those who speak but are not heard.
For those whose stories began centuries ago.
For those whose testimonies are deemed a false witness.
For those who have nowhere to turn for rest.
For those who refuse to be silenced.
For those who whisper tenderly and knowingly to their kin.
For those who shout a holy protest to their oppressors.
For those who wonder if there's any point.
For those who cannot keep truth to themselves.
For those who wail for all that has been lost.
For those who sing for all that we might become.
For those who call others to rise.
For those whose voice reaches out
like open arms for the hurting.
May they be nourished in body in soul.
May they be guided in wisdom.
May community uphold them.
Through the lips of prophets your Kindom draws near.

M Jade Kaiser, enfleshed

A Prayer for a Mass Shooting
before You Know What Is Going On

God, I believe that there have been moments
when our ancestors came to you for courage,
wisdom, fortitude, stamina, comfort, and grace.
And, I believe that coming to you did them some good.

I believe that our ancestors came to you for miracles.
I'm not a poet or a psalmist, God.
I'm not a mystic, and I don't really understand your world.
I don't know about miracles.
I feel my limitations very acutely right now.

I don't know if it's your power, God,
but if the shooting is still happening,
please do what you can to make it stop.
For the hearts that are still beating right now,
please slow down the bleeding.
Grant your children who most need it
the moments for help to arrive.

Please grant courage to the people who signed on
knowing they may confront mass shootings and terror.

Please grant courage for the people who never signed on
to confront terror and are confronting it anyway.

When the time comes, grant us wisdom, fortitude and stamina.
All of us will need wisdom, fortitude and stamina
to heal the broken world.

For today, grant comfort to everyone who feels
the pain of this moment,
whether nearby or far away.

And, God, when my children leave the dark, silent corner
furthest away from the door, grant them the grace
to see the good in the world.

Esther Teverovsky

A Prayer for the Sin of Racism

Sovereign Lord Jesus Christ, who took human form
and broke down the walls that divide;
We seek your forgiveness for not living out the truth
that all are one in Christ,
for the sin of racism.
We pray for all those affected by the marginalisation of prejudice
and the violence of racist words and actions.
We pray that we might uproot its cancerous and systemic hold
on our own institutions.
We pray that we might recognise in reverence
your divine image and likeness in our neighbour,
And find joy in the resemblance.
We pray in your name and seeking your glory. Amen.

Justin Welby and Sanjee Perera

A Prayer for an Election

Holy God
One yet Three
Reach into the abundance of your companionship
Bring forth unity and healing in our land
Cover this election with fairness and dignity
Dismantle voter suppression and intimidation
Grant simple, safe, equal access to the polls
Make the way for all voices to be heard
All votes to be counted
Cover this election with grace and integrity
Protect the process from corruption
Strengthen all working for an honorable election
Make the way for all voices to be valued
All results to be trustworthy

167

Cover this election with compassion and hope
As we await results and move into a new era
Soften and soothe hard, violent hearts
Rain down generosity of spirit
and a commitment to the common good
So all may know blessing and opportunity and belonging.
Amen.

Lisa Ann Moss Degrenia

A Prayer in a Time of Natural Disaster

O God, you divided the waters of chaos at creation.
In Christ you stilled storms, raised the dead,
and vanquished demonic powers.
Tame the earthquake, wind, and fire,
and all forces that defy control or shock us by their fury.
Keep us from calling disaster your justice.
Help us, in good times and in distress,
to trust your mercy and yield to your power,
this day and forever.
Amen.

Andy Langford

A Prayer in Times of Disaster

God of compassion,
keep vigil with us this day.
We grieve for the dead
and pray for the wounded.
We watch and wait with those
who seek news about loved ones.
We remember those who serve others—

rescue workers and police officers,
nurses and physicians,
and volunteers of every kind.
Fill them with your breath of life
as they bind up the brokenhearted,
heal bodies, and bury the dead.
Enfold us all in your tender care
as we entrust our lives to you;
through Jesus Christ our Lord. Amen.

Book of Common Worship

A Prayer for World Unity

O God, you love justice
and you establish peace on earth.
We bring before you the disunity of today's world:
the absurd violence, and the many wars,
which are breaking the courage of the peoples of the world;
militarism and the armaments race,
which are threatening life on the planet;
human greed and injustice,
which breed hatred and strife.
Send your Spirit and renew the face of the earth;
teach us to be compassionate
toward the whole human family;
strengthen the will of all those who fight
for justice and for peace;
lead all nations into the path of peace,
and give us that peace
which the world cannot give.
Amen.

Book of Common Worship

A Prayer for Peace

O God,
it is your will to hold both heaven and earth
in a single peace.
Let the design of your great love
shine on the waste of our wraths and sorrows,
and give peace to your Church,
peace among nations,
peace in our homes, and peace in our hearts.

A New Zealand Prayer Book – He Karakia Mihinare o Aotearoa

A Prayer for Racial Justice

Save us, O God, from ourselves,
from racism often cloaked in pious words,
from the machinations of white supremacy
hidden in calls for civility,
from micro aggressions thinly veiled in arrogance,
from apologies when they don't give way to action,
from forgiveness without facing the truth,
from reconciliation without reparation.
Deliver us, O God, from expecting siblings of color
to continue to bear this emotional work,
which is not theirs to do.
Grateful for the long arc that bends toward justice, we pray:
Grant us wisdom,
give us courage for the facing of these days,
by the power of the Spirit,
all for the sake of the kin-dom that we share in Christ Jesus.
Amen.

Evangelical Lutheran Church in America

A Prayer for Refugees and Migrants

Lord God, you cross every border
between divinity and humanity
to make your home with us.
Help us to recognize your face
in the refugee family,
seeking safety and protection;
in the migrant worker,
bringing food to our tables;
in the asylum-seeker,
seeking security and compassion;
in the unaccompanied child,
traveling in a dangerous world.
By the gift of your Holy Spirit,
encourage and empower us
to cross borders of our own—
showing kindness, seeking justice,
offering welcome, giving shelter.
This we pray in the name of the one
who fled as a child to Egypt,
Jesus Christ our Lord. Amen.

Book of Common Worship

A Prayer for Climate Justice

Creating God,
You have called us to be in loving relations with all the earth,
living with respect in creation,
choosing love and seeking justice at all times.
Instead, humankind has acted in hateful ways,
exploiting natural resources,
choosing power and seeking wealth in the present
over future abundance.

We need your help to fight for a better future!
Help to reawaken our love for Creation,
that is so magnificent that we,
with all our creativity and knowledge,
could never articulate it;
and so passionate that we,
with the personal price and communal cost,
would still fight for it.
Help to deepen our relationships and love for one another:
Affirming the wisdom of youth strikers,
so that we are not discouraged
by empty platitudes and naysayers; and
Growing our community of allies,
so that we can create a sustainable and faithful response
to the imminent climate crisis.
For the sake of your majestic creation, and
for the love of all our relations.
Help us to fight for a better future.
Amen.

Alydia Smith

LIST OF SOURCES

PART 1: STRUCTURES AND SEASONS

"The Basic Pattern of Worship," *The United Methodist Book of Worship* (Nashville: The United Methodist Publishing House, 1992), adapted.

"The Rhythms of Worship: The Christian Year," *The United Methodist Book of Worship* (Nashville: The United Methodist Publishing House, 1992), adapted.

"Praying in the Style of a Collect," *The United Methodist Book of Worship* (Nashville: The United Methodist Publishing House, 1992), adapted.

PART 2: WORSHIP ON THE LORD'S DAY

RESOURCES FOR PASTORS: BAPTISM

"The Baptismal Covenant II-A: A Brief Order of Holy Baptism for Children and Others Unable to Answer for Themselves," *The United Methodist Book of Worship Pastor's Pocket Edition* (Nashville: The United Methodist Publishing House, 1994), adapted.

"A Celebration of a Renewed Believer through Testimony and Baptismal Reaffirmation," *The United Methodist Book of Worship* (Nashville: The United Methodist Publishing House, 1992); "New Service of Reaffirmation of the Baptismal Covenant," Discipleship Ministries of The United Methodist Church, Copyright © 2009, https://www.umcdiscipleship.org/resources/new-service-of-reaffirmation-of-the-baptismal-covenant, and Nelson Cowan, Copyright © 2023.

Steve Garnaas-Holmes, "A Prayer Following Remembrance of Baptism," #212 in *Worship & Song Worship Resources* (Nashville: Abingdon Press, 2011).

RESOURCES FOR PASTORS: HOLY COMMUNION

"An Alternative Great Thanksgiving for General Use," *The United Methodist Book of Worship* (Nashville: The United Methodist Publishing House, 1992).

"A Concise Great Thanksgiving for General Use," Nelson Cowan, Copyright © 2023, and *The United Methodist Book of Worship* (Nashville: The United Methodist Publishing House, 1992).

"An Intergenerational Great Thanksgiving," Michelle L. Whitlock, Copyright © 2022.

RESOURCES FOR ALL MINISTERS

Words for Gathering

A: Nelson Cowan, Copyright © 2016.

B: *Reformed Worship* (Mar. 2001), 59:16, © 2001, Faith Alive Christian Resources/CRCNA. Used by permission.

C: New Revised Standard Version Updated Edition. Copyright © 2021 National Council of Churches of Christ in the United States of America. Used by permission.

D: Cláudio Carvalhaes et al., *Liturgies from Below: Praying with People at the Ends of the World* (Nashville: Abingdon Press, 2020), 38.

E: John W. Howell, *Touch Holiness: Resources for Worship, Updated*, Ruth C. Duck and Maren C. Tirabassi, eds., (Cleveland: The Pilgrim Press, 2012), 185.

F: M. Enid Watson, *Touch Holiness: Resources for Worship, Updated*, Ruth C. Duck and Maren C. Tirabassi, eds., (Cleveland: The Pilgrim Press, 2012), 192.

G: Nelson Cowan, Copyright © 2017.

H: Nelson Cowan, Copyright © 2017.

Opening Prayers / Invocations

A: *The Book of Common Prayer*, 1979, public domain.

B: The Common English Bible (Nashville: Abingdon Press, 2011), altered.

C: *The United Methodist Book of Worship* (Nashville: The United Methodist Publishing House, 1992).

D: From *Book of Common Worship*, page 906. © 2018 Westminster John Knox Press. Used by permission.

E: *Sarum Breviary*, Reprinted from *The Book of OFFICES and SERVICES of The Order of Saint Luke*, Copyright © 2012 by The Order of Saint Luke. Used by permission of OSL Publications.

List of Sources

F: Public Domain, *The Worship Sourcebook, 2nd edition* (Grand Rapids: Faith Alive Christian Resources, 2013).

G: Kwasi I. Kena, *The Africana Worship Book, Year A*, Valerie Bridgeman Davis and Safiya Fosua, eds., (Nashville: Discipleship Resources, 2006), 53.

H: Marilyn E. Thornton, *The Africana Worship Book, Year A*, Valerie Bridgeman Davis and Safiya Fosua, eds., (Nashville: Discipleship Resources, 2006), 56.

I: Ancient Collects and Other Prayers, #52 in *Worship & Song Worship Resources* (Nashville: Abingdon Press, 2011).

J: *The Book of Worship for Church and Home* (Nashville: Board of Publication of The Methodist Church, Inc., 1965), altered.

K: *The Book of Common Prayer*, 1979, public domain.

L: © *1992 The Hymnal Project*. Used by permission of Brethren Press (www.brethrenpress.com).

M: Cláudio Carvalhaes et al., "The God That Provides," *Liturgies from Below: Praying with People at the Ends of the World* (Nashville: Abingdon Press, 2020), 42.

N: Nelson Cowan, Copyright © 2022.

O: Rev. Delana Taylor, Copyright © 2020, used by permission.

P: Kwasi I. Kena, *The Africana Worship Book, Year C*, Valerie Bridgeman Davis and Safiya Fosua, eds., (Nashville: Discipleship Resources, 2008), 87.

Q: Constance Cherry, #67 in *Worship & Song Worship Resources* (Nashville: Abingdon Press, 2011).

R: "Prayer of John Chrysostom," #412 in *The United Methodist Hymnal* (Nashville: The United Methodist Publishing House, 1989).

S: Ruth Duck, *Touch Holiness: Resources for Worship, Updated*, Ruth C. Duck and Maren C. Tirabassi, eds., (Cleveland: The Pilgrim Press, 2012), 209.

T: James H. Hill, *Touch Holiness: Resources for Worship, Updated*, Ruth C. Duck and Maren C. Tirabassi, eds., (Cleveland: The Pilgrim Press, 2012), 226.

Creeds and Affirmations of Faith

"The Nicene Creed," #880 in *The United Methodist Hymnal* (Nashville: The United Methodist Publishing House, 1989).

"The Apostles' Creed, Traditional Version," #881 in *The United Methodist Hymnal* (Nashville: The United Methodist Publishing House, 1989).

"The Apostles' Creed, Ecumenical Version," #882 in *The United Methodist Hymnal* (Nashville: The United Methodist Publishing House, 1989).

Land Acknowledgements

The Greater Northwest Circle of Indigenous Ministries, "Land Acknowledgements" and "General Guidelines for Writing a Land Acknowledgment," The Pacific Northwest Conference of The United Methodist Church. Used by permission of Allen Buck.

A: Unknown origin. Many land acknowledgements derive from processes of mutual borrowing. This one is often attributed to All Saints Episcopal Indian Mission of Minneapolis, MN, but after contacting this community, they do not claim original authorship.

B: Liturgy from Native American Ministries Sunday, ResourceUMC.org, Copyright © 2021.

Prayers for Illumination

A: *The United Methodist Book of Worship* (Nashville: The United Methodist Publishing House, 1992).

B: Valerie Bridgeman Davis, *The Africana Worship Book, Year A*, Valerie Bridgeman Davis and Safiya Fosua, eds., (Nashville: Discipleship Resources, 2006), 175.

C: Brian Wren, #75 in *Worship & Song Worship Resources* (Nashville: Abingdon Press, 2011).

D: Ann B. Day, *Touch Holiness: Resources for Worship, Updated*, Ruth C. Duck and Maren C. Tirabassi, eds., (Cleveland: The Pilgrim Press, 2012), 230.

E: "Prayer for Illumination, Service IV-B," Reprinted from *The Book of OFFICES and SERVICES of The Order of Saint Luke*, Copyright © 2012 by The Order of Saint Luke. Used by permission of OSL Publications.

F: Nelson Cowan, Copyright © 2017.

Prayers of Confession

A: *Mozarabic Sacramentary*, Reprinted from *The Book of OFFICES and SERVICES of The Order of Saint Luke*, Copyright © 2012 by The Order of Saint Luke. Used by permission of OSL Publications.

B: Tony Peterson, "O Lord, We Forget You (Phil. 1:3-5)," in *The Africana Worship Book, Year C*, Valerie Bridgeman Davis and Safiya Fosua, eds., (Nashville: Discipleship Resources, 2008), 141.

List of Sources

C: Safiya Fosua, *The Africana Worship Book, Year A*, Valerie Bridgeman Davis and Safiya Fosua, eds., (Nashville: Discipleship Resources, 2006), 151-52.

D: United Church of Christ, Office for Church Life and Leadership, #86 in *Worship & Song Worship Resources* (Nashville: Abingdon Press, 2011).

E: Steve Garnaas-Holmes, #92 in *Worship & Song Worship Resources* (Nashville: Abingdon Press, 2011).

F: *Supplement to the Book of Common Prayer*, alt., Reprinted from *The Book of OFFICES and SERVICES of The Order of Saint Luke*, Copyright © 2012 by The Order of Saint Luke. Used by permission of OSL Publications.

G: The Church Pension Fund, 1998, alt. Taylor Burton-Edwards, Reprinted from *The Book of OFFICES and SERVICES of The Order of Saint Luke*, Copyright © 2012 by The Order of Saint Luke. Used by permission of OSL Publications.

Pastoral Prayers and Intercessions

A: Ruth Duck, "A Prayer for Peace and Justice (John 3:17)," *Touch Holiness: Resources for Worship, Updated*, Ruth C. Duck and Maren C. Tirabassi, eds., (Cleveland: The Pilgrim Press, 2012), 243-44.

B: Ruth Duck, "Prayer of Intercession: Losing, Seeking, Finding (Luke 15)," *Touch Holiness: Resources for Worship, Updated*, Ruth C. Duck and Maren C. Tirabassi, eds., (Cleveland: The Pilgrim Press, 2012), 149-50.

C: Dan Benedict, Reprinted from *The Book of OFFICES and SERVICES of The Order of Saint Luke*, Copyright © 2012 by The Order of Saint Luke. Used by permission of OSL Publications.

D: Sharletta M. Green, "Send a Healing Word (Lamentations 3:19-26)," *The Africana Worship Book, Year C*, Valerie Bridgeman Davis and Safiya Fosua, eds., (Nashville: Discipleship Resources, 2008), 107.

E: Ciona Rouse, *The Africana Worship Book, Year A*, Valerie Bridgeman Davis and Safiya Fosua, eds., (Nashville: Discipleship Resources, 2006), 123.

F: *The Book of Common Prayer*, alt., *The United Methodist Book of Worship* (Nashville: The United Methodist Publishing House, 1992).

G: Brian Wren, #193 in *Worship & Song Worship Resources* (Nashville: Abingdon Press, 2011).

177

Variations on the Lord's Prayer

"The Lord's Prayer, Traditional," #895 in *The United Methodist Hymnal* (Nashville: The United Methodist Publishing House, 1989).

"The Lord's Prayer, Ecumenical," English translations of The Lord's Prayer, © 1998 English Language Liturgical Consultation (ELLC), and used by permission. www.englishtexts.org.

"The New Zealand Anglican Lord's Prayer," *A New Zealand Prayerbook – He Karakia Mihinare o Aotearoa*, used by permission. Extract from *Prayer at Night's Approaching* by Jim Cotter is Copyright © Jim Cotter 2001 published by Cairns Publications and is reproduced by permission of Hymns Ancient & Modern Ltd, rights@hymnsam.co.uk.

"The Lord's Prayer (Matthew 6:9-13, First Nations Version)," Scripture quotations are taken from First Nations Version, Copyright © 2021 by Rain Ministries Inc. Used by permission of InterVarsity Press, Downers Grove, IL. All rights reserved.

Prayers of Lament

A: Lisa Hancock, "Litany for Welcoming Our Lament," adapted with permission from "Out of the Ashes: A Service of Lament in a Season of Disaffiliation," Discipleship Ministries of The United Methodist Church, Copyright © 2023.

B: Cláudio Carvalhaes et al., *Liturgies from Below: Praying with People at the Ends of the World* (Nashville: Abingdon Press, 2020), 263.

C: Author Unknown, published anonymously in #ResistHarm, A United Methodist movement of faithful resistance to anti-LGBTQIA+ policies and practice. www.resistharm.com.

Offering Prayers

A: *Banquet of Praise: A Book of Worship Resources, Hymns and Songs* by Bread for the World, 1990.

B: Herb Mather, #103 in *Worship & Song Worship Resources* (Nashville: Abingdon Press, 2011).

C: Brian Wren, #113 in *Worship & Song Worship Resources* (Nashville: Abingdon Press, 2011).

D: David Bell, #128 in *Worship & Song Worship Resources* (Nashville: Abingdon Press, 2011).

E: Cynthia A. Bond Hopson, "21st Century Africana Worship Resources for the Fifth Sunday in Lent, Year B," Discipleship Ministries of The United Methodist Church, 2007.

Invitations to Christian Discipleship

A: Valerie Bridgeman Davis, "Call to Discipleship (Based on 1 Peter 1:3-9)," *The Africana Worship Book, Year A*, Valerie Bridgeman Davis and Safiya Fosua, eds., (Nashville: Discipleship Resources, 2006), 181.

B: Dimitri of Rostov, Russia, "An Invitation to Christ," #466 in *The United Methodist Hymnal* (Nashville: The United Methodist Publishing House, 1989).

Dismissals, Blessings, and Closing Prayers

A: 2 Corinthians 13:13, The Common English Bible (Nashville: Abingdon Press, 2011).

B: Colossians 3:16a, alt., Reprinted from *The Book of OFFICES and SERVICES of The Order of Saint Luke*, Copyright © 2012 by The Order of Saint Luke. Used by permission of OSL Publications.

C: Hebrews 13:20-21, New Revised Standard Version Updated Edition. Copyright © 2021 National Council of Churches of Christ in the United States of America. Used by permission.

D: Numbers 6:24-26, alt., Reprinted from *The Book of OFFICES and SERVICES of The Order of Saint Luke*, Copyright © 2012 by The Order of Saint Luke. Used by permission of OSL Publications.

E: 1 Peter 5:10, alt., Reprinted from *The Book of OFFICES and SERVICES of The Order of Saint Luke*, Copyright © 2012 by The Order of Saint Luke. Used by permission of OSL Publications.

F: Philippians 4:4-7, alt., Reprinted from *The Book of OFFICES and SERVICES of The Order of Saint Luke*, Copyright © 2012 by The Order of Saint Luke. Used by permission of OSL Publications.

G: *The United Methodist Book of Worship* (Nashville: The United Methodist Publishing House, 1992), adapted.

H: Valerie Bridgeman Davis, *The Africana Worship Book, Year C*, Valerie Bridgeman Davis and Safiya Fosua, eds., (Nashville: Discipleship Resources, 2008), 164.

I: Junius Dotson, *The Africana Worship Book, Year A*, Valerie Bridgeman Davis and Safiya Fosua, eds., (Nashville: Discipleship Resources, 2006), 197.

J: Eugene Blair, *The Africana Worship Book, Year A*, Valerie Bridgeman Davis and Safiya Fosua, eds., (Nashville: Discipleship Resources, 2006), 199.

K: Cláudio Carvalhaes et al., *Liturgies from Below: Praying with People at the Ends of the World* (Nashville: Abingdon Press, 2020), 47.

L: Cláudio Carvalhaes et al., *Liturgies from Below: Praying with People at the Ends of the World* (Nashville: Abingdon Press, 2020), 57.

M: *Worship in Daily Life*, 1999, Discipleship Resources, #160 in *Worship & Song Worship Resources* (Nashville: Abingdon Press, 2011).

N: Kate McIlhagga, Wild Goose Publications, 1996, #169 in *Worship & Song Worship Resources* (Nashville: Abingdon Press, 2011).

O: *The Westminster Hymnal*, Continuum International Publishing Group, 2000, #173 in *Worship & Song Worship Resources* (Nashville: Abingdon Press, 2011).

P: James T. Fatzinger, *Touch Holiness: Resources for Worship, Updated*, Ruth C. Duck and Maren C. Tirabassi, eds., (Cleveland: The Pilgrim Press, 2012), 270.

Q: *The Book of Common Prayer*, alt., Reprinted from *The Book of OFFICES and SERVICES of The Order of Saint Luke*, Copyright © 2012 by The Order of Saint Luke. Used by permission of OSL Publications.

R: Alcuin of York, Reprinted from *The Book of OFFICES and SERVICES of The Order of Saint Luke*, Copyright © 2012 by The Order of Saint Luke. Used by permission of OSL Publications.

S: St. Columba, Reprinted from *The Book of OFFICES and SERVICES of The Order of Saint Luke*, Copyright © 2012 by The Order of Saint Luke. Used by permission of OSL Publications.

T: Traditional Navajo Prayer, alt., *The United Methodist Book of Worship* (Nashville: The United Methodist Publishing House, 1992).

U: Unknown.

Other Acts of Worship on the Lord's Day

Stacy Cole Wilson, "Prayer for Church Receiving New Clergy Leader(s)," *The Africana Worship Book, Year C*, Valerie Bridgeman Davis and Safiya Fosua, eds., (Nashville: Discipleship Resources, 2008), 168.

"A Covenant Prayer in the Wesleyan Tradition," #607 in *The United Methodist Hymnal* (Nashville: The United Methodist Publishing House, 1989).

PART 3: WORSHIP ANY TIME OR PLACE

RESOURCES FOR PASTORS

"A Service of Committal," The United Methodist Book of Worship (Nashville: The United Methodist Publishing House, 1992), adapted by Nelson Cowan, with an addition from *Renewing Worship, Volume 4. Life Passages: Marriage, Healing, Funeral* (Minneapolis: Augsburg Fortress Press, 2002), used by permission.

"A Service of Word and Table V with Persons Who Are Sick or Homebound," *The United Methodist Book of Worship* (Nashville: The United Methodist Publishing House, 1992).

Robin Knowles Wallace, "Great Thanksgiving for Communion in Times of Crisis," *Just in Time: Communion Services* (Nashville: Abingdon Press, 2006).

John Gill, "Commissioning and Blessing of Newly Licensed Foster Parents," Copyright © 2013, adapted with permission by Lisa Ann Moss Degrenia and Nelson Cowan.

Perrin Crouch, "Covenant Affirmation after an Autism Diagnosis," Copyright © 2020.

"An Order for the Installation of Church Leaders," *The United Methodist Book of Worship* (Nashville: The United Methodist Publishing House, 1992).

"Prayer for Godspeed: A Service of Farewell for Departing Members," Copyright © 1994, Reformed Church Press; used and adapted with permission.

"A Service for the Blessing of Animals," *The United Methodist Book of Worship* (Nashville: The United Methodist Publishing House, 1992), adapted by Nelson Cowan, with additions from Maren C. Tirabassi, *Touch Holiness: Resources for Worship, Updated*, Ruth C. Duck and Maren C. Tirabassi, eds., (Cleveland: The Pilgrim Press, 2012), 199, and Barbara Allen.

"A Service for the Blessing of a Home," *The United Methodist Book of Worship* (Nashville: The United Methodist Publishing House, 1992), adapted.

RESOURCES FOR ALL MINISTERS

Rhythms of the Calendar Year

Ruth Duck, "Beginning a New Year (Heb. 11:1-2 and Phil. 3:12-15)," *Touch Holiness: Resources for Worship, Updated*, Ruth C. Duck and Maren C. Tirabassi, eds., (Cleveland: The Pilgrim Press, 2012), 228.

"For Martin Luther King Jr. Day," Untitled prayer of Martin Luther King Jr., Coretta Scott King Collection, In Private Hands, Sermon file, folder 97. Reprinted by arrangement with The Heirs to the Estate of Martin Luther King Jr., c/o Writers House as agent for the proprietor New York, NY. Copyright © 1953 by Dr. Martin Luther King, Jr. Renewed © 1981 by Coretta Scott King.

Ken Carter, "Earth Day Prayer of Confession," Copyright © 2005.

Jon Humphries, "For Mother's Day," Copyright © 2019.

Doug Paysour, "For Memorial Day," originally published as "A Prayer of Remembrance," Ministry Matters, Copyright © 2013.

"For Father's Day," Unknown author, *Prayers of The Church of England*, public domain.

"Juneteenth: A Pouring of Libations," *Worship Resources: Juneteenth*, Copyright © 2019 Evangelical Lutheran Church in America, used by permission.

Steve Garnaas-Holmes, "Prayer for Our Country" *Unfolding Light: Daily Reflections and Worship Resources* (blog), Copyright © 2023.

Andy Langford, "For Independence Day," *The United Methodist Book of Worship* (Nashville: The United Methodist Publishing House, 1992).

Marilyn E. Thornton, "Back to School Blessing," *The Africana Worship Book, Year C*, Valerie Bridgeman Davis and Safiya Fosua, eds., (Nashville: Discipleship Resources, 2008), 166.

Copyright © Marcia McFee, "A Blessing of the Backpacks (Intergenerational)."

United Methodist Communications, "A Blessing for Workers and All Seeking Work," Copyright © 2015.

The Episcopal Church Office of Indigenous Ministries, "For Indigenous Peoples' Day," 2012, adapted with permission.

"For Veterans Day," *Prayer Book for the Armed Services*, Evangelical Lutheran Worship (Minneapolis: Augsburg Fortress Press, 2013), 65, used by permission.

Diana Butler Bass, "A Thanksgiving Prayer: Choose Gratitude," *The Cottage* (blog), Copyright © 2020, https://dianabutlerbass.substack.com.

Lisa Ann Moss Degrenia, "Recognizing the Longest Night at Home," Copyright © 2022. www.revlisad.com.

List of Sources

Waking and Sleeping

Ken Carter, "An Examen in the Wesleyan Tradition," Copyright © 2020.

"O Gracious Light (Phos Hilaron)," *The Book of Common Prayer*, 1979, public domain.

"A Prayer before Sleeping (A)," *Mozarabic Sacramentary*, Reprinted from *The Book of OFFICES and SERVICES of The Order of Saint Luke*, Copyright © 2012 by The Order of Saint Luke. Used by permission of OSL Publications.

John Henry Newman, "A Prayer before Sleeping (B)," Reprinted from *The Book of OFFICES and SERVICES of The Order of Saint Luke*, Copyright © 2012 by The Order of Saint Luke. Used by permission of OSL Publications.

Dan Benedict, "A Prayer upon Waking (A)," Reprinted from *The Book of OFFICES and SERVICES of The Order of Saint Luke*, Copyright © 2012 by The Order of Saint Luke. Used by permission of OSL Publications.

Peter Millar, "A Prayer upon Waking (B)," #217 in *Worship & Song Worship Resources* (Nashville: Abingdon Press, 2011).

"A Prayer upon Waking (C)," *The Book of Common Prayer*, 1979, public domain.

Interpersonal Prayers / Blessings

"A Blessing for a Wedding Engagement," from *Inclusive Marriage Services: A Wedding Sourcebook*, page 168. © 2015 Westminster John Knox Press. Used by permission.

"A Blessing for Newlyweds," from *Inclusive Marriage Services: A Wedding Sourcebook*, page 135. © 2015 Westminster John Knox Press. Used by permission.

"An Anniversary Blessing," from *Inclusive Marriage Services: A Wedding Sourcebook*, page 180. © 2015 Westminster John Knox Press. Used by permission.

"A Prayer for Someone Going through a Divorce," *The United Methodist Book of Worship* (Nashville: The United Methodist Publishing House, 1992).

The Book of Common Prayer, "A Prayer for Wisdom," *The United Methodist Book of Worship* (Nashville: The United Methodist Publishing House, 1992).

Native American, "A Prayer for Peaceable Conversations," #207 in *Worship & Song Worship Resources* (Nashville: Abingdon Press, 2011).

Kate Mackereth Fulton, "A Prayer for Tough Conversations," *Speaking Truth: Women Raise Their Voices in Prayer*, J. Paige Boyer et al., eds., (Nashville: Abingdon Press, 2020), 55.

Nelson Cowan, "A Prayer for After an Argument," Copyright © 2023.

Copyright © Lisa Ann Moss Degrenia, "A Prayer for Irreconcilable Differences."

Michael J. O'Donnell, "A Prayer for Forgiveness," Reprinted from *The Book of OFFICES and SERVICES of The Order of Saint Luke*, Copyright © 2012 by The Order of Saint Luke. Used by permission of OSL Publications.

Nelson Cowan, "A Prayer for a Friendship that has Ended," Copyright © 2023.

Healing and Wholeness

"A Service of Healing," adapted from *The United Methodist Book of Worship* (Nashville: The United Methodist Publishing House, 1992), and *The United Methodist Hymnal* (Nashville: The United Methodist Publishing House, 1989).

"A Prayer for One Who Knows They Will Never Be Fully Well Again," from *A Barclay Prayer Book*, page 284. © 2003 The Estate of William Barclay. Used by permission of Westminster John Knox Press.

David Sparks and Sheila Noyes, "A Prayer for Living Fully in the Dying Days," *The United Church of Canada/L'Église Unie du Canada*. Used by permission. Source: https://united-church.ca/worship-theme/death-and-dying.

"A Prayer for the Courage to Move on from the Past," attributed to St. Augustine of Hippo, public domain.

"A Prayer in Times of Worry," attributed to Martin Luther, public domain.

"A Prayer for Those Who Mourn," #461 in *The United Methodist Hymnal* (Nashville: The United Methodist Publishing House, 1989).

"A Prayer for the Loss of a Child," *The United Methodist Book of Worship* (Nashville: The United Methodist Publishing House, 1992).

"God of the Living" © Jan Richardson from *The Cure for Sorrow: A Book of Blessings for Times of Grief*. Used by permission. janrichardson.com.

Carol Penner, "Prayer for Those Addicted to Drugs," Copyright © 2018. www.leadinginworship.com Used by permission.

List of Sources

"A Service for the Loss of a Beloved Pet," *Journal of the General Convention of The Episcopal Church*, Indianapolis, pages 719-721, and *Enriching Our Worship 1*, Copyright © 1998 by The Church Pension Fund.

Leadership and Church Life

"A Prayer of Commissioning for Missionaries or a Mission Team," *The Book of Occasional Services 2018*, The Episcopal Church.

Copyright © Steve Garnaas-Holmes, "A Prayer for the Consecration of a Building, or Celebration of a Remodel."

Copyright © Steve Garnaas-Holmes, "A Prayer for Church Discernment."

Copyright © Marcia McFee, "A Covenant to Precede Difficult Conversations."

Safiya Fosua, "A Prayer during Change," #198 in *Worship & Song Worship Resources* (Nashville: Abingdon Press, 2011).

Peter Wyatt, "A Prayer for Those Leaving Our Church," #206 in *Worship & Song Worship Resources* (Nashville: Abingdon Press, 2011).

Mark W. Stamm, "A Collect for The United Methodist Church," Copyright © 2020.

Nelson Cowan, "A Prayer for Those Who Find Themselves without a Church," Copyright © 2023.

Nelson Cowan, "A Prayer for Pastoral Leadership during Holy Week," Copyright © 2022.

Nelson Cowan, "A Prayer for Those with Imposter Syndrome," Copyright © 2021.

Walter Brueggeman, "A Prayer for Singing," #185 in *Worship & Song Worship Resources* (Nashville: Abingdon Press, 2011).

Nelson Cowan, "A Prayer before a Budget Meeting," Copyright © 2023.

Drew Weseman, "A Prayer for Quilting Groups," Copyright © 2023.

Copyright © Kate Mackereth Fulton, "A Prayer for the Ending of a Longtime Church Ministry."

Family and Home

Drew Weseman, "A Prayer before Baking Bread," Copyright © 2023.

Drew Weseman, "A Prayer before Preparing a Meal," Copyright © 2023.

"A Prayer for Enjoying Wine," *The Book of Occasional Services 2018*, The Episcopal Church.

Table Blessing A, Traditional.

Table Blessing B, #621 in *The United Methodist Hymnal* (Nashville: The United Methodist Publishing House, 1989).

Table Blessing C, *The Book of Common Prayer*, 1979, public domain, adapted.

Table Blessing D, Prayers written and compiled by presbytery Hunger Action Advocates Copyright Presbyterian Church (U.S.A.), A Corporation.

Table Blessing E, Traditional Lutheran.

Table Blessing F, "The World Hunger Grace," Author Unknown.

"A Brief Prayer of Blessing of a Home," *The Book of Occasional Services 2018*, The Episcopal Church.

"A Prayer for [a] New Parent[s]," *A New Zealand Prayerbook – He Karakia Mihinare o Aotearoa*, used by permission.

Copyright © Angela Rotherham, "A Blessing for an Adoption."

"A Prayer for Help to Conceive or to Accept Infertility," *Enriching Our Worship 5: Liturgies and Prayers Related to Childbearing, Childbirth, and Loss*, Copyright © 2009 by The Church Pension Fund.

"A Prayer for Letting Go the Hope of Childbearing," *Enriching Our Worship 5: Liturgies and Prayers Related to Childbearing, Childbirth, and Loss*, Copyright © 2009 by The Church Pension Fund.

Prayers of the Saints

"A Prayer of Saint Patrick," *The United Methodist Book of Worship* (Nashville: The United Methodist Publishing House, 1992).

"A Prayer of Susanna Wesley," *The United Methodist Book of Worship* (Nashville: The United Methodist Publishing House, 1992).

"A Prayer of St. Francis of Assisi," #481 in *The United Methodist Hymnal* (Nashville: The United Methodist Publishing House, 1989).

Labor, Vocation, Hobbies

R. DeAndre Johnson, "A Prayer for Today," *Yes and Amen: A Prayer Collection*, featuring artwork by Ibraim Nascimento, Copyright © 2023, used by permission.

List of Sources

Keri K. Wehlander, "A Prayer of Discernment for an Individual," originally published as "A Turning Season," *Circles of Grace: Worship and Prayer in the Everyday* (Toronto: United Church Publishing House, 1998).

Copyright © Andrea Hunter and Katie Ritsema-Roelofs, "A Prayer When Work is Scarce," *Worship for Workers: Worship Resources for All Those Who Labor*. www.worshipforworkers.com.

Safiyah Fosua, "A Blessing for Active Military Leaving for Deployment," originally published as "A Prayer for Protection of Those in Military Service," 2003, "Praying for Peace in the Face of War: Resources for Worship," Discipleship Ministries of The United Methodist Church, Copyright © 2010.

"A Prayer for Caregivers," *Evangelical Lutheran Worship* (Minneapolis: Augsburg Fortress Press, 2006), used by permission.

"A Prayer for Health Care Providers," *Evangelical Lutheran Worship* (Minneapolis: Augsburg Fortress Press, 2006), used by permission.

"A Prayer for First Responders," Excerpts from the English translation of Book of Blessings © 1987, International Commission on English in the Liturgy Corporation. All rights reserved.

"A Blessing for Educational Institutions," *A New Zealand Prayerbook – He Karakia Mihinare o Aotearoa*, used by permission.

Ruth Duck, "A Blessing for a Time of Sabbatical," *Touch Holiness: Resources for Worship, Updated*, Ruth C. Duck and Maren C. Tirabassi, eds., (Cleveland: The Pilgrim Press, 2012), 176.

"A Prayer for Artists and Musicians," *The Book of Common Prayer*, 1979, public domain.

Nelson Cowan, "A Prayer to Appreciate the Pauses in Life," Copyright © 2023.

Copyright © Robert Elsner, "A Prayer for Engaging a Prayer Labyrinth."

Copyright © Steve Garnaas-Holmes, "A Prayer for a Garden."

Copyright © Marcia McFee, "A Prayer for Travel."

Copyright © W. David O. Taylor, "A Prayer for Going on Vacation."

Affirmation and Inclusion

"A Blessing for Someone Who Embodies a New Name," *Pastoral Liturgies for Journeys of Gender Affirmation and Transition. Rites and prayers supplemental to the Book of Alternative Services*, The Anglican Church of Canada, 2023, used by permission.

"A Prayer of Affirmation for Gender Transition" *Pastoral Liturgies for Journeys of Gender Affirmation and Transition. Rites and prayers supplemental to the Book of Alternative Services*, The Anglican Church of Canada, 2023, used by permission.

"Help Us Find Beauty Within Ourselves" by Rev. Dr. Kenji Marui. © 2021 The United Church of Canada. Used by permission. *This prayer was created for the 40 Days of Engagement on Anti-Racism for The United Church of Canada.* Source: https://united-church.ca/prayers/help-us-find-beauty-within-ourselves.

"A Prayer for the World and Its Peoples," Church of Scotland, alt., *The United Methodist Book of Worship* (Nashville: The United Methodist Publishing House, 1992).

Amanda Larsen, "A Prayer of Thanksgiving for All," adapted with permission from Scott Roberts, "Prayer for Friendship Sunday, 2017," https://network.crcna.org/topic/justice-inclusion/disability-concerns/attitudes/prayer-friendship-sunday-2017.

"A Prayer of Welcome after an Absence from Church," *The Book of Occasional Services 2018*, The Episcopal Church.

Eleanor Colvin, "A Prayer for Someone Who Should Not Need to Be Resilient," Copyright © 2023.

Justice and Peace

Bill Sinkford, "An Interfaith Prayer for Justice," in Kayla Parker, *Becoming: A Spiritual Guide for Navigating Adulthood* (Boston: Skinner House Books, 2015).

The Rev. Dr. Jerry Maynard (The People's Priest), "A Prayer before Attending a Demonstration," *The Episcopal Street Action Handbook*, Copyright © 2020 The Episcopal Church, eds., Rev. Dr. Jerry Maynard and Rev. Melanie Mullen.

Rev. M Jade Kaiser, "A Prayer for the Lips of Prophets," enfleshed: spiritual nourishment for collective liberation. www.enfleshed.com.

Esther Teverovsky, MD, "A Prayer for a Mass Shooting, Before You Know What is Going On," originally published on Ritualwell.org, used by permission.

"A Prayer for the Sin of Racism," originally published as "A Prayer for Racial Justice Sunday," Archbishop Justin Welby and Canon Dr. Sanjee Perera, Copyright © 2021, used by permission.

List of Sources

Lisa Ann Moss Degrenia, "A Prayer for an Election," Copyright © 2020. www. revlisad.com.

Andy Langford, "A Prayer in a Time of Natural Disaster," *The United Methodist Book of Worship* (Nashville: The United Methodist Publishing House, 1992).

"A Prayer in Times of Disaster," from *Book of Common Worship*, page 626. © 2018 Westminster John Knox Press. Used by permission.

"A Prayer for World Unity," from *Book of Common Worship*, page 627-628. © 2018 Westminster John Knox Press. Used by permission.

"A Prayer for Peace," *A New Zealand Prayerbook – He Karakia Mihinare o Aotearoa,* used by permission.

"A Prayer for Racial Justice," *Evangelical Lutheran Worship* (Minneapolis: Augsburg Fortress Press, 2006), used by permission.

"A Prayer for Refugees and Migrants," from *Book of Common Worship*, page 630-631. © 2018 Westminster John Knox Press. Used by permission.

Alydia Smith, "A Prayer for Climate Justice," originally published as "A prayer for the Fridays for Future Climate Strike movement," *The United Church of Canada/L'Église Unie du Canada*. Used by permission. Source: https:// united-church.ca/prayers/help-reawaken-our-love-creation.

LIST OF
CONTRIBUTORS

The following persons generously contributed some of the content for this volume:

Eleanor Colvin (she/her) serves in the Texas Conference of The United Methodist Church. A Blessing for Someone Who Should Not Need to Be Resilient

Perrin Crouch (she/her) serves as a deacon in the Missouri Conference of The United Methodist Church. Covenant Affirmation after an Autism Diagnosis

Lisa Ann Moss Degrenia (she/her) serves in the Florida Conference of The United Methodist Church and writes at www. revlisad.com. Recognizing the Longest Night at Home; A Prayer for an Election; A Prayer for Irreconcilable Differences; Commissioning and Blessing of Newly Licensed Foster Parents

Robert Elsner (he/him) serves as Professor and Chair of Psychology at Samford University in Birmingham, Alabama. A Prayer for Engaging a Prayer Labyrinth

Kate Mackereth Fulton (she/they) serves in the Baltimore-Washington Conference of The United Methodist Church. A Prayer for Tough Conversations; A Prayer for the Ending of a Longtime Church Ministry

Steve Garnaas-Holmes (he/him) is a retired United Methodist pastor living in Maine, who blogs at unfoldinglight.net. A Prayer for a Garden; A Prayer for the Consecration of a Building, or Celebration of a Remodel; A Prayer for Church Discernment

Lisa Hancock (she/her) serves at Discipleship Ministries of The United Methodist Church. Litany for Welcoming Our Lament

R. DeAndre Johnson (he/him) serves in the Texas Conference of The United Methodist Church. A Prayer for Today

Marcia McFee (she/her) is the Creator and Visionary of Worship Design Studio www.worshipdesignstudio.com. A Blessing of the Backpacks; A Covenant to Precede Difficult Conversations; A Prayer for Travel

Drew Weseman (he/him) serves in both the Florida Conference and the Michigan Conference of The United Methodist Church and writes at www.sabbathbaking.com. A Prayer for Quilting Group; A Prayer before Baking Bread; A Prayer before Preparing a Meal

Michelle L. Whitlock (she/her) serves in the Susquehanna Conference of The United Methodist Church. An Intergenerational Great Thanksgiving

Please visit
www.abingdonpress.com/worshipanytimeorplace
to find the following helpful content:

Appendix A provides a glossary of Christian symbols. These symbols provide meaningful connections for people and can be used in formal and informal times of worship. Well-prepared worship leaders of all types understand the significance of these words and symbols. Illustrations are included.

Appendix B provides a guide to vestments (attire for leaders) in worship. Who should wear a robe or stole or chasuble, and when? And what does a chasuble look like? This appendix explains multiple options and includes illustrations.